Shakespea

A 146-mile Footpath between Shakespeare's Birthplace, Stratford-upon-Avon and Shakespeare's Globe, London

CONTENTS

INTRODUCTORY SECTION

CHAPTERS

Published by:
The Macmillan Way Association
on behalf of:
The Shakespeare's Way Association,
St Mary's Barn, Pillerton Priors,
Warwick CV35 0PG

First published
January 2006

ISBN 0-9526851-6-7

Front Cover Photograph:
Our Path beyond Marsh Baldon
(see page 37)

Introducing Shakespeare's Way

Using existing foot-paths, bridleways and a few minor roads where absolutely necessary, this 146-mile `long-distance` footpath has been planned to follow, as closely as possible, a route that Shakespeare may have taken on some of his journeys back and forth between his home town and the city in which he spent most of his productive years. Shakespeare's Way provides a fine walk

The Royal Shakespeare Theatre, Stratford-upon-Avon

between the poet's birthplace at Stratford-upon-Avon and Shakespeare's Globe, London. Passing over the Oxfordshire Cotswolds and the Chilterns, and going beside the Thames, it links some of Britain's best-loved tourist destinations - Stratford-upon-Avon itself, Blenheim Palace, Oxford and London. Passing within a mile or two of Heathrow Airport it could also provide an unspoilt walking route for those passengers who wish to go eastwards into London or, more importantly, north-westwards to Oxford and Shakespeare's Stratford.

While its main objective is to offer a good walk its planners also hope to raise funds for Stratford-upon-Avon's Shakespeare Hospice (Registered Charity No. 1064091), a vitally important facility which is funded almost entirely by charitable donations. We shall do this by encouraging walkers to raise funds by obtaining sponsorship from friends, relations and work colleagues and we shall also pass all profit on the sale of our guidebooks to the same organisation.

The Route of Shakespeare's Way

Shakespeare's Way follows a route that the poet may have taken on his journeys between Stratford-upon-Avon and London (*we shall explain the reasons for our choice later*). First we go southwards, up the valley of the River Stour, a little river which empties into the Avon just below Stratford. We leave the Stour at a point not far from its source to the east of Cherington and climb up onto the limestone of the Oxfordshire Cotswolds just beyond Long Compton. On high country we pass close to the mysterious Rollright Stones and enter Oxfordshire going over rolling country to the busy market town of Chipping Norton. From here we go over hill country, now often punctuated by quiet wooded valleys, and then through the parkland of Ditchley before walking through Capability Brown's magnificently landscaped Blenheim Park.

We then go through Woodstock, the lovely stone town at Blenheim's gate, before walking through Bladon churchyard, beside the modest tombstone of Britain's greatest statesman, Sir Winston Churchill. Beyond here we walk through woodlands and across fields to Yarnton, with its attractive church; and then briefly beside the Oxford Canal ("no canal in William's time", we hear you say!) to Wolvercote where we join the Thames flowing southwards beside the great expanse of Port Meadow and into Oxford. Hoping to persuade you to linger awhile in this finest of all university towns, we take you past the site of an inn almost certainly used by Shakespeare, before we re-join the Thames by Folly Bridge.

Walking beside the river we pass the line of college boathouses and Iffley's interesting Norman church, but at Sandford-

The River Stour beyond Alderminster (see page 12)

on-Thames we leave the river and head across country, leaving the southern suburbs of Oxford behind. And now across quiet country through which the River Thame flows, through a number of unspoilt villages and up onto the beech woods of the chalk-formed Chilterns. We cross several south-running valleys as we switchback across the Chilterns into Buckinghamshire before dropping down to the Thames again, at busy little Marlow. We go beside the ever-widening river, past Bourne End and as far as Stanley Spencer's beloved Cookham. Here we leave the river once again and head across sandy Buckinghamshire heathland, following an existing footpath - the Beeches Way. We go right through the great woodlands of Burnham Beeches and further wooded areas now classified as Country Parks before arriving at Iver, on London's western fringe.

As an introduction to the busy London world we cross the extraordinarily noisy M25 - it looks and sounds even worse from a footbridge, than it does from a vehicle! But beyond the noise we return to sanity by joining the Grand Union Canal (again we hear you say "no canal in William's time", but there is no walking alternative if London is to be reached). We now use the canal towpath all the way to Brentford, a quiet route, a level route, but rather a bland one, except for the stretch beside the Hanwell Flight of Locks. At Brentford we re-join the Thames, following the north bank as far as Kew Bridge and then the south bank all the way to Shakespeare's Globe, passing many points of interest on the way.

Our path beyond Willington (see page 16)

3

How to Use this Guide

This guide to the 146-mile-long Shakespeare's Way is in three parts: The first, an introductory section giving some of the background to its creation and use, the second, a detailed description of the path itself, divided into five chapters, and the third, providing information on Shakespeare's early years and his journeys between Stratford and London. The Key Map inside the front cover shows the coverage of each chapter while the contents are shown on the Title Page, including the map content of each chapter.

Each of the 33 double-page spreads is entirely self-contained, with map, text and illustration all inter-relating. This will ensure that when the book is opened out and inserted into a transparent map case, it can stay there until the next map section is reached. The maps are at a scale of 1:50,000 (about one-and-a-quarter inches to the mile) and are based upon the Ordnance Survey's Landranger series. The sheet numbers of the Ordnance Survey's Landranger and Explorer maps covering the area similar to that covered by each of our own maps are also indicated and there is a chart on page 7 showing the OS maps covering the route.

The symbols and signs used on the maps are shown in the block below.

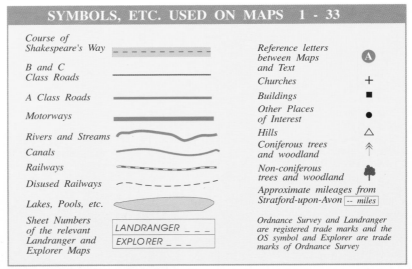

SYMBOLS, ETC. USED ON MAPS 1 - 33

Course of Shakespeare's Way	
B and C Class Roads	
A Class Roads	
Motorways	
Rivers and Streams	
Canals	
Railways	
Disused Railways	
Lakes, Pools, etc.	
Sheet Numbers of the relevant Landranger and Explorer Maps	LANDRANGER _ _ _ EXPLORER _ _ _

Reference letters between Maps and Text	Ⓐ
Churches	+
Buildings	■
Other Places of Interest	●
Hills	△
Coniferous trees and woodland	
Non-coniferous trees and woodland	
Approximate mileages from Stratford-upon-Avon	-- miles

Ordnance Survey and Landranger are registered trade marks and the OS symbol and Explorer are trade marks of Ordnance Survey

Each paragraph of text starts with a reference letter and this cross-refers with the same letter on the accompanying map. All information not concerned with the actual route directions is shown in italics, while the route details themselves are in normal type. It will also be noted that progressive mileages from Stratford-upon-Avon are clearly displayed on every map and this will allow users to work out very simply the distance between any two points. It will also enable users to see how far they have gone and there is also a chart on page 74 showing the distances from both Stratford-upon-Avon and Shakespeare's Globe. Free Update Sheets to cover any amendments to route details are available from us at the address shown on the opposite page.

Accommodation details are constantly changing and are not therefore included in this guide. However, details of B&Bs, hotels, inns and camping sites will be found in the small frequently up-dated supplementary leaflet, *The Shakespeare's Way Planner*, which is available from the Shakespeare's Way Association, St Mary's Barn, Pillerton Priors, Warwick CV35 0PG. Please send a cheque *(made payable to the Shakespeare's Way Association)* for £2.75, all of which will be passed directly to the Shakespeare Hospice of Stratford-upon-Avon (if you wished to send more it would be gratefully received!).

With the help of information in this guidebook it should be possible to follow Shakespeare's Way without further guidance. However, the route from Stratford-upon-Avon to Shakespeare's Globe is also waymarked with Shakespeare's Way waymarks, apart from sections using public roads and where we use the Thames Path and the Grand Union Canal, where it is unnecessary. The waymarks are of two types - a self-contained plastic roundel with arrow and Shakespeare's Way logo and a self-adhesive sticker with Shakespeare's Way logo, which is stuck on a standard yellow or blue waymark arrow (yellow for footpath and blue for bridleway). We hope that you have no difficulties, but if any are encountered it would be appreciated if you could let us have the details - *The Shakespeare's Way Association, St Mary's Barn, Pillerton Priors, Warwick CV35 0PG.* This will help us maintain the existing trail and improve it where necessary.

Walk Shakespeare's Way and support the Shakespeare Hospice - Registered Charity No. 1064091

Shakespeare's Way has been developed to forge an interesting link between Stratford-upon-Avon and London and to raise funds for Stratford's Shakespeare Hospice. This is an independent care centre offering palliative care to people living with a life-threatening illness in Stratford-upon-Avon and South Warwickshire. Based in Shottery near Stratford-upon-Avon, their Day Care Service supports the whole family, offering a range of therapies and health care ranging from pain and symptom control, spiritual care and complementary therapies, to counselling and support groups for carers.

Their 'Hospice at Home' team, also based at the hospice, cares for those people who wish to die at home, surrounded by their loved ones. Sometimes patients do not have any immediate family and this is when the hospice nurse becomes the most important person, helping the patient in the last weeks of their life, knowing that they are not alone. In many cases the hospice staff have long-term relationships with patients, when they can enjoy and rediscover their life at the hospice. It is not uncommon for people to be discharged and so hope is an important part of our holistic approach to palliative care.

As the Shakespeare Hospice is an independent charity with minimal government support, they rely on the generosity and support of the community. This comes in a wide variety of ways but we are especially hoping that our pathway will also help to raise funds for the Shakespeare Hospice and with this in mind, might we suggest that you 'sponsor' yourselves for a small sum per mile and ask your friends and relations to help out by also becoming your sponsors. We can provide appropriate Sponsorship Forms. If you require one please write to us: The

Shakespeare's Way Association, St Mary's Barn, Pillerton Priors, Warwick CV35 0PG. When you have finished your walk we can, should you so wish, let you have a Certificate of Congratulations. If you have managed to collect some sponsorship money (either from yourself, or from your friends and relations), this would of course be gratefully acknowledged on your Certificate.

A Countryside Code for Shakespeare's Way Walkers

Be safe - **plan ahead** and follow signs. Be prepared for the unexpected. Please

respect the working life of the countryside, as our actions can affect people's livelihoods, our heritage, and the safety and welfare of animals and ourselves. Keep to public paths across farmland *and walk in single file to minimise path-spread or crop damage.* Use gates and stiles to cross fences, hedges and walls. **Leave gates and property as you find them**. **Take your litter home** (*nice thought, but if you are some days away from home, dump it in a litter bin in the next village you pass through*). Don't forget that litter is not only untidy, but it can also cause great harm to animals and farm machinery. Make sure you don't harm animals, birds, plants or trees. **Keep dogs under close control,** *keeping them on leads when there is any chance of encountering stock. Don't forget that pregnant ewes are very much at risk even from merely playful dogs.* It is your duty to ensure that your dog is not a danger or a nuisance to farm animals, wildlife or other people. Take special care on country roads, *usually walk towards oncoming traffic, but on blind bends walk on the outside of the bend where you will be most visible.* Make no

Woodland near Hambleden (see page 46)

unnecessary noise. Show consideration for other people and help to make the countryside a pleasant place for all, at home, at work or at leisure.

A Friendly Countryside for All

While planning Shakespeare's Way and its sister paths, the Macmillan Ways, we have received great kindness from many land owners and tenant farmers and we have assured them that walkers along our path will go quietly through their land and that you will not give offence. If you look at things from country people's point of view, they are far more likely to appreciate yours.

When meeting anyone on your journey, take time to stop and pass the time of day with them. Many farmers and farm workers to whom we have talked, say how surprised they are by the number of walkers who just plod by without even saying hello. Stop to talk and you could well learn so much more about the country through which you are passing. Don't be discouraged if you don't always get a response, but keep trying - the overall result will be well worthwhile, and the next Shakespeare's Way walkers that come along are more likely to have a friendly welcome. We have all got to live together, so please - let co-operation be your watchword, rather than confrontation. You won't regret it.

ORDNANCE SURVEY MAP COVERAGE OF SHAKESPEARE'S WAY

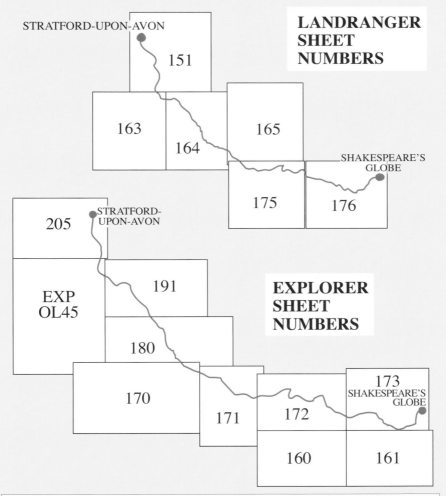

The Chart above indicates the Sheet Numbers of both the Landranger and Explorer Maps covering the route of Shakespeare's Way. Landranger maps are at an approximate scale of one and a quarter inches to the mile while the Explorer Maps are at an approximate scale of two and a half inches to the mile. It is hoped that in their future editions, these maps will show the exact route. However it should be possible to make do with the maps and route directions in this guidebook. They are at the same scale as the Landranger maps, upon which they are based.

Chapter 1   Stratford-upon-Avon to Chipping Norton

(A) Having visited the Shakespeare Centre and the adjoining Shakespeare's Birthplace (*he was born here in 1564, his father, John, being a prosperous glover and wool dealer - for further details of his early years and our theorising on his journeys to and from London, see pages 75-77*), head south-eastwards along Henley Street towards the centre of the town marked by a building topped by a white cupola, which is occupied by Barclay's Bank. Turn right at central roundabout overlooked by this bank, cross entry to Wood Street and go along right-hand side of High Street. Pass Harvard House (*the home of the ancestors of John Harvard, whose will resulted in the foundation of Harvard University which now owns this house*) and the Garrick Inn, both on right and over cross-roads by Town Hall to left, with a statue of Shakespeare given by the actor David Garrick, in a niche above its handsome porch. Now go along Chapel Street, crossing road to left-hand pavement and passing the Shakespeare Hotel on left.

Pass the interesting Nash's House on left and the foundations of New Place just beyond. *The latter was purchased by Shakespeare in 1597 and he died there in April 1616. Sadly it was demolished in 1759. Visible just beyond the foundations is an Elizabethan-style Knot Garden and beyond this is the most attractive Great Garden (see below).* Turn left into Chapel Lane by the Guild Chapel (but go straight ahead for a few yards if you wish to look at some of the original buildings of King Edward VI's School on left, almost certainly Shakespeare's place of learning). Now go down Chapel Lane, passing entry to the Great Garden, of New Place, on left, the modern buildings of King Edward VI's School on right and a second entry to the Great Garden on left (*don't miss a visit here*).

(B) At the bottom of Chapel Lane, turn right into Waterside where entrance to the Swan Theatre is immediately ahead. (*To visit the Royal Shakespeare Theatre turn left and continue along Waterside, the theatre now being on your right. Return along left-hand side of road in front of the Swan Theatre to rejoin main route.*) Veer left to enter gardens immediately beyond the Swan Theatre and then veer right to go along path to immediate right of river bank. Fine views down the river to Holy Trinity Church ahead. At end of lawn veer right, then left to go on path between low fence on left and low wall on right. The Black Swan Inn (usually known as the Dirty Duck) visible back right, across road at this point. Pass ferry point on left and keep straight up path heading for circular end of pavilion, now occupied by a Brass Rubbing Centre. River still just alongside on left. Beyond Brass Rubbing Centre keep beside river along pathway overhung with bushes. Veer to right by massive tree and head along path just to left of public toilets. Leave gardens and turn left onto pavement beside road passing a *Welcome to Stratford* notice board. Enter churchyard of Holy Trinity Church - the burial place of William Shakespeare. Go up paved pathway between avenue of lime trees and pass to immediate right of north porch (*but do go inside, for quite apart from its Shakespearean connection it is a most handsome building*). Continue around the west end of the church, soon leave churchyard and continue in same direction, going along pavement on left-hand side of road. At end of road and immediately beyond entry to Lucy's Mill (flats) go down surfaced pathway with River Avon soon visible to left.

Shakespeare's Birthplace

(C) Immediately before large road-bridge ahead, turn left to cross river by concrete footbridge. Then turn right onto path going beneath road-bridge and immediately beyond, turn left to go down path running parallel with noisy road on embankment above to left and with wooden fence to right. After about 100 yards turn right to go over stile and head across field on well-defined path, soon starting to go uphill between fence on left and (initially) hedge on right. At top of hill, fence on both sides of path. Through small gate and keep on path. Through metal kissing gate and keep in same direction, now on wide track. *Clifford Chambers church visible ahead and well beyond it is Ilmington Hill.* Turn left through metal kissing gate where track veers to right and go across short strip of field.

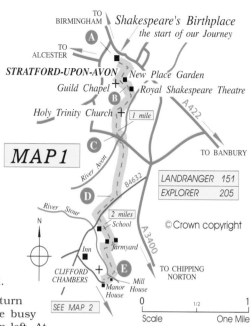

(D) Through metal kissing gate and turn right to walk down boring path beside busy B4632. Pass entry to Clifford Park on left. At bottom of small hill turn left **to cross road with great care** to follow sign to Clifford Forge House. Go along surfaced roadway with wall to right. Pass early 19th-century house on right (part of school) and converted barns, also on right. Keep through rougher farmyard with modern barns on both sides and just beyond, turn right to go down track with fence on left and wooden stables on right. At end of track, with metal gate ahead, turn left onto fenced path. Over stile and veer slightly right across field aiming for squeeze-stile in fence-line ahead with a few small trees. Through squeeze-stile and keep in same direction across next, smaller field.

(E) Soon turn right to go across substantial footbridge over a branch of the River Stour, the valley of which we shall be following for about 17 miles. Through metal gate and immediately turn right onto narrow path with river on right. Turn left with pool on left and follow grassy track to go in front of the old watermill (now a house) crossing the main branch of the Stour, flowing beneath the mill. Keep on fenced path as it turns to right and through small wooden gate beside large wooden gate to enter the attractive village of Clifford Chambers.

Holy Trinity Church,
Stratford-upon-Avon

9

(A) At entry to Clifford Chambers turn right to go beside attractive green to left by gates of beautiful Clifford Manor, largely re-built by renowned architect, Sir Edwin Lutyens, soon after World War I. After 40 paces turn left, initially to go along short driveway used by long mellow-brick house called *Palings* and then straight ahead onto grassy track beyond. (*But go straight ahead if you wish to visit the church with its thin Perpendicular tower and its chancel over-restored by the Victorians or the New Inn about 400 yards beyond, at the far end of the village.*) Turn left at T-junction of tracks and go along tree-bordered

House below the church, Preston-on-Stour

path. Soon go across farm road onto narrow path with fence on right and holly hedge on left. At end of path keep in same direction on grassy track across large open fields (*but first look back, left to see brick-built gazebo - the work of Sir Edwin Lutyens we presume*). *The dumpy spire of Atherstone-on-Stour Church soon visible ahead.* Through very wide gap in cross-hedge and keep in same direction, now on smooth-surfaced farm track (*caution - this can be very slippery after rain - the compiler came to grief here!*).

(B) Pass large barn on right and bear left onto public road in minute Atherstone-on-Stour. Pass Victorian church on left (*now in private hands*) and pass barns converted into offices, with timber-yard just beyond, both on left. Where road bends to left to cross River Stour, turn right, off road, onto track immediately beyond thatched cottage. *Good views over to left of handsome early-Gothic-Revival mansion, Alscot Park, around which we are now going to skirt.* Up this short track and along left-hand edge of field. Bear slightly left near top of field to go over small ditch and keep along left-hand edge of field, with wood to immediate left. Turn left at corner of wood to follow edge of wood on left and another field to right. At end of wood go over stile to left beside large wooden gate with mound to our immediate left (*No, it's not prehistoric - but is thought to be the prosaic remains of a summer-house's foundations!*). Bear right to follow well-used path across undulating field with good views over to left of Alscot Park and the meandering River Stour.

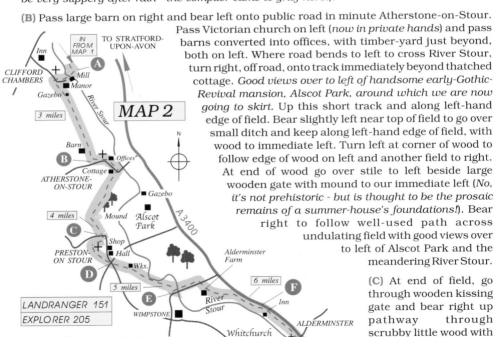

(C) At end of field, go through wooden kissing gate and bear right up pathway through scrubby little wood with nettles, soon joining end of surfaced public road at entry to Preston-on-

10

Stour. Pass *The Old Vicarage* on left and soon turn right to follow path up right-hand edge of attractive village green overlooked by timbered and mellow-brick houses, with low garden wall to immediate right. Cross roadway and go through handsome wrought-iron gates into churchyard. Go up yew-shaded path and skirt around the right-hand side of the church. Go out of churchyard through gate opposite west door of church. (*But spare a few minutes to visit this delightful church. Apart from the east and west windows, all the others have plain glass and light floods in on the plain oak pews and the many handsome wall monuments to members of the West family of Alscot Park, most of which are in the chancel. There is also a balcony and a fine 20th-century crucifix in memory of Sir Michael West. Don't overlook the excellent copy of Hereford Cathedral's Mappa Mundi in the porch below the west tower.*) Turn left after leaving churchyard keeping to right of churchyard wall, passing terrace of colourful cottages on right and keep in same direction down wide green. Note useful village shop down to left. There may also be a tearoom next-door to it. Now veer right onto public road by Village Hall on left and leave village.

(D) Go straight over cross-roads and through wooden kissing gate. Head straight across field going just to right of low buildings of sewage works. Through gateway to immediate right of sewage works and follow to immediate right of works fence. Veer slightly right across field, aiming to right-hand end of projecting hedge. On reaching hedge, follow to its immediate right. River Stour just beyond hedge to left at this point, before it meanders away further to left. Near end of field cut across corner, heading for just visible metal bridge in cross-hedge, with willow trees ahead. Cross bridge over the ditch-like Humber Brook and go across next field aiming just to left of transformer on power-pole. Turn right by transformer and small pumping station on right and follow track on immediate right. River Stour, with bridge across it, now just to left.

(E) Over stile beside wooden gate and turn left to follow public road over bridge crossing River Stour for the second time. **Go along this road with great care keeping to right-hand side of road to face oncoming traffic except on bends when you should go on their outside to give traffic as much warning of your presence as possible.** After about 400 yards turn right to go along surfaced farm road. Just before reaching low brick building on right turn left to follow around fenced lawn, soon turning right. Beyond fencing, go through gap in hedge ahead and veer slightly right to go across Alderminster Farm's driveway and through large metal gate. Go diagonally across large field initially aiming for point where fence goes up bank to possible stile in hedge bordering main road. Go over concrete 'bridge' across possibly dry ditch and veer slightly right to aim for small stile in middle of cross-fence ahead, thereby ignoring initial direction. Over this stile and keep along top of bank with the Stour in field below to right and with

Bridge over the Stour at Point E

hedge to left shielding some of the noise from main road just beyond. Keep along path through bushy area with hedge never far away to left.

(F) Before reaching power-pole turn left to go over stile close to 30MPH sign before turning right to go along path beside the very busy A3400 at the entrance to Alderminster village. *It is regretted that the next mile will be noisy and irritating, but there is no viable alternative. It would no doubt have been rather more tranquil in Shakespeare's day!*

(A) Pass row of 19th-century estate houses on right. Pass The Bell Inn on right and note the width of the verges beyond, *which owe their existence to the horse-drawn Stratford and Moreton Tramway, which opened in 1826; closing less than 50 years later.* Pass Alderminster Church on right. *Although much restored in the 19th century, the splendid interior proportions of the earlier building have been retained.* Pass car parking area just beyond churchyard. *If you feel like a rest here, walk down to right and take short path back, right, beside the River Stour where there is a very welcome bench.* Soon bear right, off A3400 just beyond Old School on right onto quieter old road passing mellow-brick Howard's End on right with its attractive clock-face. Soon re-join A3400 keeping on path.

(B) Just beyond Bridge House, bear right down tree-shaded path to go over bridge crossing River Stour. Go straight across large field aiming just to left of terrace of houses well ahead. Through metal kissing gate with Stour just alongside to left and keep in same direction across next field now heading for gateway in corner of field well to left of terrace of houses.

(C) Through metal kissing gate to left of large gate and turn left onto minor public road immediately passing Crimscote entry sign. *(We shall now be on roads for well over two miles, but regrettably there is no alternative.)* Pass Blacksmith's Barn on left and, just beyond, a view through gateway to left of lovely old dovecote (Private). Turn left at road junction (SP - *Newbold*) and go uphill on road leaving Crimscote. Keep on road with parkland now on both sides. Talton House now visible over to left. Keep along road as it bends to left with entrance gates to Talton House on left. Turn left at road junction with iron fence to left and keep along road with pool and parkland to left. Pass Talton Mill Farm Shop *(ice creams, drinks, etc.)* and go over two bridges crossing branches of River Stour. Pass Sea Scout Hut on right.

(D) After 50 paces go over offset cross-roads **crossing busy A3400 with great care** to go onto minor road by main entrance to Ettington Park Hotel (SP - *Ettington*). Pass minor entrance to hotel on right with glimpse of hotel through trees. *If you are interested in architecture do try to visit it. Built between 1858 and 1862 it is a fine example of the High-Victorian style. The exterior is embellished with extravagant sculptural detail, much of which illustrates events in the history of the family who built it - the Shirleys. It **may** also be possible, **with permission**, to visit the private chapel in the gardens of the hotel. This, the first of Ettington's churches, dates from about 1100. The 12th-century tower has survived and the south transept is now a private memorial chapel for the Shirley family and contains a series of Shirley memorials and has a particularly fine 20th-century stained-glass east window.* Woods of Ettington Park now on right for some time. Up slope beyond small brick bridge, still keeping on road. Pass entry to 'Business Park' on right and eventually woods on both sides of road.

Howard's End, Alderminster

Woods on left side cease and bear right keeping on road before dropping down hill with woods again on both sides. Turn right, off road; go through or beside large wooden gates and down farm track with woods on right. Follow track as it starts to drop gently down and bends to right twice. Now turn left at junction of tracks by possible hay/straw storage area on left.

Spire of Tredington Church soon visible some distance ahead. Brailes Hill, with its clump of trees, visible ahead left and the line of the Oxfordshire Cotswolds in the far distance beyond. Keep on track as it bends to right and then left. Parkland and garden of Ettington Park to right - no access to hotel or old church from this track. Keep on track as it drops down into valley and starts to go gently up across large field (part of the old park) soon bearing slightly to left. Now head up track going between two pairs of ancient oak trees. *Good view of Newbold-on-Stour Church over Stour Valley to right.*

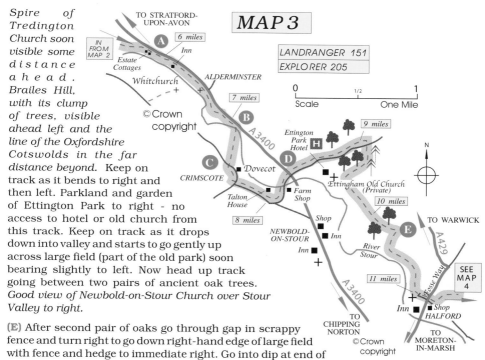

MAP 3

LANDRANGER 151
EXPLORER 205

Scale 0 1/2 1 One Mile

© Crown copyright

TO STRATFORD-UPON-AVON
IN FROM MAP 2
6 miles
Inn
Estate Cottages
Whitchurch
ALDERMINSTER
7 miles
A 3400
9 miles
Ettington Park Hotel
Dovecot
CRIMSCOTE
Talton House
Farm Shop
Ettingham Old Church (Private)
10 miles
8 miles
Shop
NEWBOLD-ON-STOUR
Inn
Inn
River Stour
TO WARWICK
A 429
SEE MAP 4
11 miles
Fosse Way
Inn
Shop
HALFORD
TO CHIPPING NORTON
A 3400
TO MORETON-IN-MARSH
© Crown copyright

(E) After second pair of oaks go through gap in scrappy fence and turn right to go down right-hand edge of large field with fence and hedge to immediate right. Go into dip at end of first field and emerge up into second field just before turning left to follow well-defined track, sometimes used as motorcycle scrambling course. River Stour down to right, below bushy bank. *Brief glimpse ahead, right, of Halford's church tower.* Bear round to right at junction of tracks with bushes still below to right and go below low-voltage power-line. Follow track as it bends round to right but soon turn left near end of track to go across very narrow strip of field and through small wooden gate. Immediately beyond gate veer half-right across field aiming for house with pronounced gable-end and flat brick extension below, to its left. Drop down over brow and keep in same direction heading with care for the right-hand of three small wooden gates - the other two are private! Go through two gates and over sleeper bridge crossing small stream and go up gently curving pathway in miniature parkland (edged with daffodils in spring) beyond. This is known as Henry's Meadow, but is only signed as such at the far, village, end. Leave Henry's Meadow by large wooden gate and turn right onto public road at the entry to Halford village. Immediately bend to left by the Old Manor House on right. Bear left by small working smithy on left and church on right. *Although heavily restored in the 19th century this church contains several items of interest including a tympanum over the north doorway and capitals beneath, all of which are fine examples of Norman carving. There is also an attractive 16th-century font cover, topped by carvings of five bishops' heads and a single choir stall complete with a strange misericord.* Beyond church keep along quiet road, passing house on left with elegantly balustraded balcony over its porch. Bear up to right by phone box on left and then, **with great care, go straight across the very busy A429, Fosse Way**, onto the Idlicote Road. *Post Office and Halford Bridge Inn down to right before crossing road and opposite them is the Halford Garage with its very useful shop. The Fosse Way, which ran for 182 miles between Lincoln and Exeter, was built by the Romans a few years after their invasion of Britain in AD43.*

13

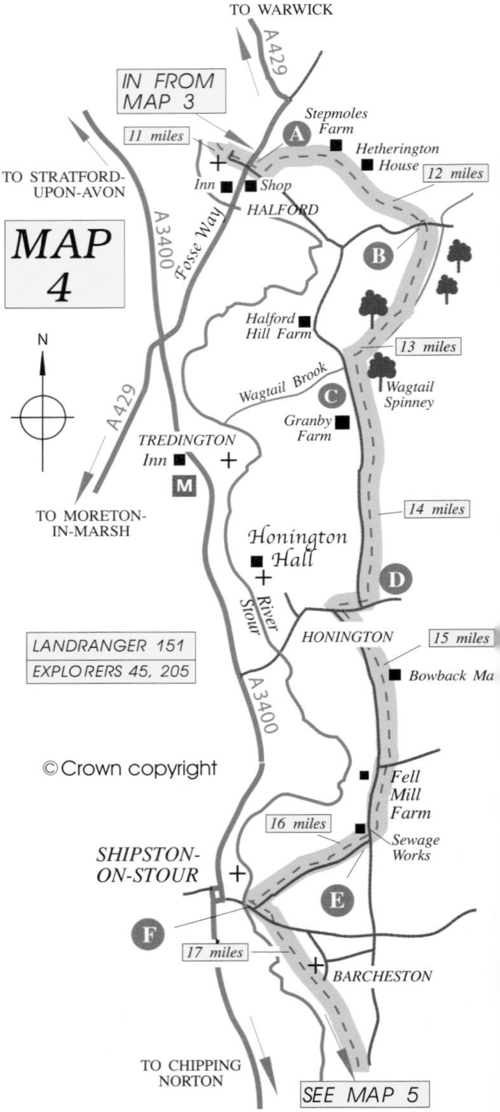

(A) Having crossed the A429, the Romans' Fosse Way, in Halford, go down Idlicote Road and pass road called The Leys on left. Just beyond useful bench on left, turn left down small road called The Close; useful bus shelter opposite bench. Turn left onto roadway immediately beyond House No 3, cross car parking area and go along pathway with Leylandii hedge to left and fence on right. Through gate and keep in same direction across field heading for indistinct stile below telephone pole. Through gate below telephone pole and turn right to go up surfaced farm drive. At top of drive bear right, off track and keep along left-hand edge of field, first passing horse-chestnut trees on left and then Stepmoles Farm, over to left followed by hedge on immediate left. Cross surfaced driveway and veer slightly right to go between probable avenue of young trees to small gate in cross-hedge. Through this gate, which is to immediate right of small spinney on edge of garden of handsome neo-Georgian Hetherington House. Now veer left to go across field, aiming for stile to right of large wooden gate. Over stile and go down right-hand edge of field with hedge on immediate right. Veer left near end of field following hedge-line and through metal gate just to left of corner. Then turn right to go through second gate before turning left onto road.

(B) After about 60 paces turn right, off public road, to go through a small metal gate. Go across field, walking parallel with the Wagtail Brook well down to left, and just to left of hedge projecting from right-hand edge of field. We shall now be following the Wagtail Brook for almost a mile. Keep in same direction beyond hedge projection and near end of field, drop down to go through small metal gate in cross-hedge. Beyond gate veer slightly right to keep to right of projecting woodlands and brook, and ignoring footbridge to left. On rounding slight bend, head for small metal gate in cross fence ahead, still keeping parallel with brook to left. Through this metal gate and go straight across corner of field on right-of-way and then follow pathway between left-hand edge of field and brook. At end of field go through metal gate onto often muddy track with woodland to right. If too difficult veer a little way left, off track. Through wide gap at end of woodland and onto track running parallel with brook to left, soon bending well to right. Brick-built bridge over brook soon visible ahead with Halford Hill Farm on bank well beyond.

TO WARWICK

IN FROM MAP 3

11 miles

TO STRATFORD-UPON-AVON

Stepmoles Farm

A

Hetherington House

12 miles

Inn ■ ■ Shop

HALFORD

MAP 4

B

N

Halford Hill Farm

13 miles

Wagtail Brook

C

Wagtail Spinney

Granby Farm

TREDINGTON Inn ■

M

TO MORETON-IN-MARSH

14 miles

Honington Hall

D

HONINGTON

15 miles

LANDRANGER 151
EXPLORERS 45, 205

River Stour

© Crown copyright

Bowback Ma

Fell Mill Farm

16 miles

Sewage Works

SHIPSTON-ON-STOUR

F

E

17 miles

BARCHESTON

TO CHIPPING NORTON

SEE MAP 5

14

(C) Through metal gate to right of bridge and turn left to go onto public road and over bridge crossing the Wagtail Brook and going up hill beyond, with Wagtail Spinney to left. *The Wagtail Brook soon joins our old friend the River Stour below this bridge, less than a mile to the south-west of this point. (Regrettably we shall now be on public roads for almost three miles, but there is no viable alternative.)* Beyond top of hill good views over to right before passing impressive Granby Farm on right. *Spire of Tredington Church visible over to right.* Pleasant road with wide grass verges.

The Wagtail Brook beyond Point B

View over to right over parkland to lovely Honington Hall. Pass Honington entry sign.

(D) Turn right at T-junction (SP - *Shipston*) and soon turn left at next road junction (SP - *Barcheston*). *(But go straight ahead if you wish to visit the very attractive village of Honington with its wide greens overlooked by many beautiful houses. Handsome late 17th-century Honington Hall (sometimes open) lies beyond the village. The elegant church beside it is largely contemporary with the Hall.)* Keep out of Honington on now slightly busier public road and beyond end of village pass Bowback Manor on left. Over bridge crossing small brook and go straight, not right, at road junction by Fell Mill on right (SP - *Barcheston*).

(E) Pass two entrances to sewage works on right and between second entrance and road junction ahead, turn right to go down wide, grassy track with sewage works fence to right. *Note reed-beds beyond fence - a comparatively new method of sewage treatment.* At end of fence go through wide gap and onto well-used path across field, veering slightly left. Through small metal gate in fence and veer right to keep in same direction, on well-used path across very large field. At end of field keep in same direction down path through plantation.

The Market Square, Shipston-on-Stour

(F) Go up concrete steps with River Stour not far to right, through gap in low wall and turn left onto public road with great care. *(But if possible turn right to cross the bridge over the River Stour to visit the lively little market-town of Shipston-on-Stour, with colourful shops and welcoming inns lining its little market square. 'Sheepstown' was once a most important market for sheep, and its variety of delightful 17th-, 18th- and 19th-century houses bear witness to a prosperity lasting many hundreds of years.)* Almost immediately ignore small road to Honington on left, but just beyond it, turn right to go through gate. Follow well-defined path across field to go over stile into next field. Continue across this next field, still on well-defined path, heading for stile below low-voltage power-pole. Over this double-stile and keep across next field veering slightly to left of power-pole line. Our old friend the River Stour down below us to right. Through metal kissing gate and go diagonally across next field to its far left-hand corner. *Barcheston Church visible over to left.*

15

(A) Over stile beside large wooden gate to enter minute hamlet of Barcheston and bear slightly left on track with hedge to right and wall to left, with Manor Farm beyond. *The present house is largely 17th-century, but it was at the manor here in about 1560 that William Sheldon set up a tapestry weaving enterprise. The best-known productions from here were the Sheldon Tapestry Maps, several of which have survived.* Keep bearing left by brick barn conversion and then turn right through large metal gate off road as it bends further to left by old cast-iron village pump on left. (B*ut walk up to left if you wish to visit Barcheston Church, with its interesting interior containing the fine 16th-century alabaster tomb of William Willington.*) Having turned right, off road, go straight across field following defined track approximately parallel with winding hedge to right. Track soon becomes well-defined footpath, going closer to hedge than previously. Over stile and sleeper bridge in cross-hedge and keep in same direction across sloping field with ridge-and-furrow still much in evidence. *In some cases ridge-and-furrow is a survival of ancient field-systems, but on clay soils such as here, this is more likely to be the result of ploughing to improve drainage.* The River Stour just below us on right. Over stile in cross-hedge and veer slightly right across next field to keep on well-defined path. At end of field go through small metal gate to immediate left of River Stour, crossed here by a farm bridge, but not by us. Go straight across track, up narrow path with hedge on left and fence on right to enter village of Willington (*no special features*).

(B) Bear slightly right on surfaced road keeping to immediate right of stone house with projecting bread-oven. Pass relatively modern houses on right and left before bearing left on road beyond Old Brook Cottages on right, ignoring footpath straight ahead. Pass Rose Barn on left and then turn right at T-junction of roads by welcome bench. Leave Willington and walk down road with care. At next road junction, just beyond Willington entry sign, go straight (SP - *Cherington*), not right. After about 300 yards turn right, off road, to go over stile and go diagonally right up across field aiming just to left of wood ahead. Through gap to immediate left of wood by remains of stile and old water-trough and keep in same direction to go diagonally up across next field aiming just to left of wood on near horizon. *Good views back towards Shipston from half-way up field.* At top of hill veer slightly left to aim down hill for almost invisible gap about 40 paces to left of small wooden hunting gate visible in corner (**not** our objective!). Arrive at 'gap' and use it to cross wooden bridge over ditch. Keep in same direction, go over stile in cross-fence and veer slightly right to go over stile in cross-hedge. Cross very narrow field, possibly laid out as miniature motorcycle scrambling course, and over another stile. Keep in same line across next field soon going parallel with hedge to right. *Large modern stone house - Burmington Grange - visible over to left.* Over stile in field corner and keep in same direction up steep little hill with hedge to immediate right.

Our path down to Cherington

(C) Over stile at end of field and turn left to go along road for about 110 paces. Then turn right through gap in hedge and go diagonally across field aiming for power-pole in far corner of field. At end of field go over stile below double power-pole and keep along top, left-hand edge of field with hedge to immediate left. Over double-stile and sleeper bridge in cross-hedge just to right of corner and go diagonally left with bridge ahead eventually coming into view.

Manor Farm

A3400

(D) Through metal gate to cross farm bridge over the River Stour - *the last time we shall see our old friend, whose valley we have been following from Clifford Chambers just beyond our start at Stratford-upon-Avon.* Ignore possible sign indicating a diverted path to spinney on right - this is not **our** path but go straight ahead along very short length of grassy track to go through a second gate. Now turn left to cross large field aiming just to left of Cherington's church tower. Through gates and over small wooden bridge and veer slightly left to cross field and keep in same direction to go over two stiles before turning right onto public road and immediately turning left by Cherington Mill with house on left (SP - *Stourton*). Soon enter pleasant stone village of Cherington and just before reaching the Cherington Arms, on left, turn right to go along right-hand edge of its car park and go along a narrow path. (*But go to left if you wish to visit the Cherington Arms.*) Go across surfaced driveway with garages on right and over stile into field. Go up across ridge-and-furrow field, aiming for centre of church. Through iron kissing gate at left-hand end of iron fence and go across churchyard keeping just to right of church and through gate, passing pathway to south door of church. *This has a well-proportioned tower, fine Perpendicular windows, some with interesting medieval glass, and a lovely 14th-century canopied tomb-chest.* Beyond gate turn left onto small road and then turn right onto wider road (SP - *Wolford*).

WILLINGTON

18 miles

TO CHIPPING NORTON

19 miles

Burmington Grange

Inn

CHERINGTON

20 miles

21 miles

0   1/2   1
Scale   One Mile

LANDRANGER 151
EXPLORER 45

N

© Crown copyright

22 miles

Margett's Hill
Farmhouse

Barns
Whichford Wood

SEE MAP 6

(E) Soon turn left up initially surfaced road opposite postbox in wall on right. Leave Cherington and go onto rougher track and keep on this as it veers slightly right and through hedge-line. Still keep on track with hedge now alongside on right. Ignore track to right and keep up track with hedge still on right. Track now has hedge on its left, rather than its right and now starting to climb steeply. Keep on track as it bends, first to left and then turns to right along contour, with hedge now on right. Beyond small spinney on left, go over stile beside metal gate, ignoring footpath sign on right. Go straight on up hill following bridleway waymark. Veer up left keeping well to left of oak tree and continue up hill with hedge over to our left. *This is our first real climb out of the Midland Plain, so stop from time to time, perhaps to draw breath and certainly to look back at the amazing view taking in Brailes Hill to the right with its clump of trees, and below, the church towers of Brailes, Sutton-under-Brailes and Cherington, and the distant line of the classic Cotswolds well over to the left.*

(F) Through metal gate and onto more defined track with hedge to immediate right. Keep on track, passing barns on left and farmhouse of Margett's Hill on right. Beyond farm keep straight along drive, which soon levels out and starts to drop very slightly. Whichford Wood now visible ahead. At end of surfaced drive turn right with care onto public road.

(A) After about 150 yards turn left off road onto track with hedge to left and woodland of Whichford Wood to right. Near bottom of slope bear right keeping on better-used track and almost immediately turn right at junction of tracks in Whichford Wood. *(From this point until paragraph D, below, we shall share our route with the Macmillan Way, a 290-mile coast-to-coast footpath between Boston and Abbotsbury. If you wish to walk from here to Boston - only 134 miles away! - go straight ahead at this junction, rather than turning right.)* However, having turned right, go down track with woodlands on both sides, continuing to drop down almost all the way to Long Compton. Keep on track into field and woodlands soon again on right. *Good view of Long Compton church tower ahead and beyond, to its left, the ridge that we shall shortly climb.* Woods on right end just before going through metal gate with overgrown stile beside it and pond visible to its left. Keep on track along left-hand side of next field with hedge to left. At end of field through gateway and keep along hedge-bordered track. Through gateway and go across field, with large pond over to left, towards large metal gate well to left of house and to right of vehicle depot. Through gate and go straight across yard.

(B) **Turn left with care** onto path on left-hand side of busy A3400 (SP - *Woodstock*), having now entered Long Compton. *Sitting below the high Cotswold edge, this village has many attractive stone houses and cottages strung out along the A3400.* Keep along A3400, passing church on right with its handsome Perpendicular tower and charming thatched lych-gate. Pass road to right, leading to camp site (3/4 mile), Manor Hotel on left, *Taste of the Country* food shop on right and Post Office shop on right. Pass bus shelter on right, school on left, turning to Butler's Lane on left, interesting Millennium Chronolog on left (*do stop to look at this*) and Village Hall on right.

(C) Immediately beyond Village Hall turn right **to cross A3400 with great care** and go through large wooden gate to immediate right of stone pillar entrance to Daddy's Bank. (*But go straight ahead for a few yards if you wish to visit the Red Lion Hotel.*) Go up short concrete roadway, leaving Long Compton and through second wooden gate. Go along short length of roadway before veering right to head across short field for stile in cross-fence. Over this stile (beside large wooden gate) and keep across next field in same direction to go over stile beside metal gate. Turn left through miniature farmyard and almost immediately turn right onto surfaced drive with hedge to right. Where drive turns to right at entry to converted barn, go straight ahead on broad grassy track with hedge still to right. Where grassy track turns right veer very slightly left to go up large field on well-defined path, eventually aiming for stile in top, left-hand corner. Go over this stile and

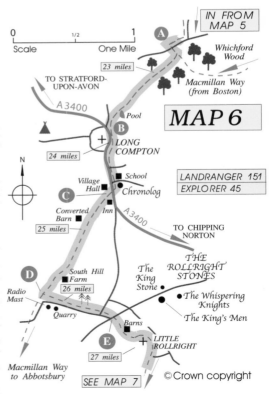

IN FROM
MAP 5

Whichford Wood

0   1/2   1
Scale   One Mile

23 miles

TO STRATFORD-
UPON-AVON

Macmillan Way
(from Boston)

A3400

Pool

MAP 6

B

LONG COMPTON

24 miles

N

Village Hall

School

Chronolog

LANDRANGER 151
EXPLORER 45

C

Converted Barn

Inn

A3400

25 miles

TO CHIPPING NORTON

THE ROLLRIGHT STONES

South Hill Farm

The King Stone

D

26 miles

Radio Mast

The Whispering Knights

Quarry

The King's Men

Barns

LITTLE ROLLRIGHT

E

27 miles

Macmillan Way
to Abbotsbury

SEE MAP 7

© Crown copyright

18

keep in same direction up next field heading just to right of waymarked post. Veer slightly left by this post (by boggy spring), soon going parallel with hedge up to right. Through small metal gate in sporadic cross-hedge and veer right to eventually come close to right-hand hedge. South Hill Farm now visible ahead. At end of field bear right, under ash tree, go over stile beside metal gate and keep up farmyard well to right of farm buildings with sporadic hedge to immediate right. At end of farmyard keep in the same direction to cross field on well-defined path aiming for gap well to right of radio mast.

(D) Over stone 'stile' in hedge and turn left with care onto minor public road, leaving the Macmillan Way. (*If you went straight on at this point you could follow the Macmillan Way all the way to Abbotsbury on the Dorset Coast - just over 150 miles ahead.*) Keep down road, which forms the border between Warwickshire and Oxfordshire, passing quarry entrance on right and then small wood on left. *Somewhere in this area we cross the watershed between the Severn and the Thames and from now on, any streams or rivers we encounter will flow south and east*

In Whichford Wood

eventually joining the Thames. The ones we crossed in previous days eventually flow into the Severn. Keep straight, not left, at road junction (SP - *Rollright Stones*). Look left for a last view of our old friend, Brailes Hill, topped by its clump of trees.

(E) After 75 yards bear slightly right at road T-junction (*but turn left and go along road for half-a-mile if you wish to visit the Rollright Stones - The King's Men, an impressive Bronze Age stone circle, The Whispering Knights, the remains of a burial chamber and The King Stone, an isolated `standing stone`*). But on main route, **go across road with great care** to go through gap to left of large metal gate and down track with sporadic hedge on left - now definitely in Oxfordshire. Chipping Norton visible on ridge well ahead. Turn right by two barns on left and almost immediately turn left off track, to go quite steeply down grassy track between avenue of young (in 2004) trees, with Little Rollright Church soon visible in valley just to left of track.

The King's Men - The Rollright Stones

(A) At entry to Little Rollright turn left at T-junction onto surfaced farm road just before reaching church. *But go ahead for 25 paces to churchyard gate if you wish to visit church. Do take time to visit this lovely little building, with its unspoilt interior illuminated by much clear glass in its windows. There are old oak pews, two fine monuments in the chancel and a quiet feeling of times past.* Follow farm road as it first bears round to left, then bears right with stone barn up to left. Keep straight past gate on right and then bend round to right going gently downhill. Ignore sign to left indicating Darcy Dalton Way which we are now joining (*now following the Darcy Dalton Way, a 65-mile path from the Oxford Canal at Wormleighton to the Ridgeway Path near Wayland's Smithy*). Soon fork right, off farm road onto path with wall on its immediate right, going gently downhill. Follow path as it bends to right, with steep grassy bank up to right. Cross small bridge over stream and, if possible go straight ahead. *(It may be necessary to first go to right, up steps, before turning left with building on left, but this is due for demolition).* Soon go up more steps

Little Rollright Church

with handrail through wide gap in hedge. Go straight up field keeping to immediate left of grassy bank. Through waymarked gap in sporadic hedge and keep along top right-hand edge of very large field with hedge to immediate right. Valley down to our left carries a small stream flowing south and west to join the Evenlode, a tributary of the Thames. At end of field through hunting gate into largely coniferous wood and keep on reasonably defined path veering left and gradually descending.

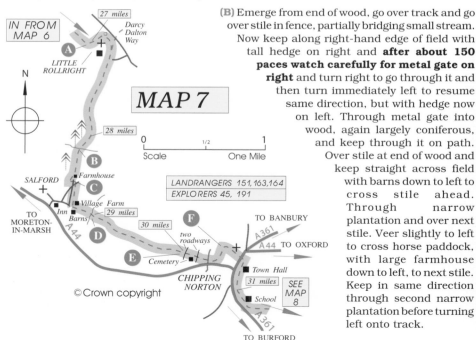

(B) Emerge from end of wood, go over track and go over stile in fence, partially bridging small stream. Now keep along right-hand edge of field with tall hedge on right and **after about 150 paces watch carefully for metal gate on right** and turn right to go through it and then turn immediately left to resume same direction, but with hedge now on left. Through metal gate into wood, again largely coniferous, and keep through it on path. Over stile at end of wood and keep straight across field with barns down to left to cross stile ahead. Through narrow plantation and over next stile. Veer slightly to left to cross horse paddock, with large farmhouse down to left, to next stile. Keep in same direction through second narrow plantation before turning left onto track.

20

(C) After 25 paces turn right onto surfaced roadway at entry to Salford village. Ignore footpath sign to left. *We have now left the Darcy Dalton Way.* Go straight across diagonal crossroads by village green and houses up to right and houses down to left. Keep down road ignoring footpath sign to left and pass turn to Orchard Close on left. Where road bends to right, turn left to go through yard of Village Farm (SP - *Chipping Norton*) (*but turn right, to go up road if you wish to visit Black Horse Inn and/or church. The latter dates almost entirely from the mid-19th century, but incorporates a few Norman features from the building it replaced*). Pass modern barns on right and garden to left and go through two large metal gates keeping on fenced track that gently curves to right.

(D) Cross small brook and soon, at end of surfaced track, go through metal gate. Keep on now grassy track veering slightly to left and starting to go gently uphill. Go over stile in cross-hedge to left of fenced gap and keep up track across this next field. At end of track at top of field go over stile and, keeping in similar direction, go up right-hand edge of next field with hedge to immediate right. At end of field go over stile in corner and veer slightly right across next field on well-defined path. Just before end of field, good views of Chipping Norton ahead as we breast this rise. Over stile in cross-hedge with industrial building visible ahead right and the chimney of the old Bliss Tweed Mill visible well beyond.

(E) Keep down right-hand edge of field to go over surfaced road bordered with trees and wide grass verge. Over stile slightly to right and keep in same direction, now on surfaced path. Pass bench commemorating Queen's Golden Jubilee on left and large cemetery over to right, ignoring path to it. Over two stiles crossing surfaced road and keep down field with bushes and trees to right and houses well over to left. Go over small stone footbridge and do **not** fork left, but keep straight ahead up steep bank. Veer left on bank and through gate. Bear left immediately beyond fenced infants' play area and head across field (partly a games pitch) in direction of church tower.

(F) Through metal kissing gate at far, right-hand end of field and turn left onto surfaced roadway. Soon turn right onto wide path by entrance to The Mount on left. Now entering Chipping Norton. Keep up roughly-surfaced path with hedge to left and wall to right. Go beside white gate into churchyard and up path, passing short path to south porch. *Do spare a moment to visit this handsome church with its finely vaulted octagonal south porch and splendidly proportioned interior. Although heavily restored this is in the best Perpendicular*

Almshouses at Chipping Norton

tradition. Do not miss the brasses displayed on the north wall nor impressive tomb chest with the alabaster figures of Thomas Rickardes and his wife, Elizabeth, who was a Fiennes of Broughton Castle. Bear slightly right up into Church Street (not named here), soon passing attractive almshouses on left. At top of Church Street turn right by the Chequers Inn to go along Market Street. Just before reaching HSBC Bank on right, turn left, up across car park and cross busy road at controlled pedestrian crossing. Then turn right to go along pavement with Market Square above to left with shops beyond. Pass Town Hall (*the work of George Repton, son of the well-known landscape designer, Humphry Repton*) on our immediate left.

Chapter 2   Chipping Norton to Oxford

(A) Keep on pavement passing Chipping Norton Town Hall on our immediate left. Go straight over first small road junction by Fox Hotel on left, but at next road junction turn left (SP - *Burford - A361*) by King's Arms Hotel. Soon bear right at next road junction (SP - *Burford*). Pass Fire Station on left and immediately beyond controlled pedestrian crossing on right and Chipping Norton School on left, bear left up pathway to immediate right of school buildings. At end of path keep in same direction down roadway with dry-stone wall on left and large Leisure Centre beyond to left. Pass tennis courts on left and extensive allotment area over to right. Track soon becomes more grassy and passes entry on right to the seven-acre William Fowler Memorial Wood, planted with broadleaf trees in winter of 2001/2002. Through kissing gate to left of large metal gate and keep in same direction on now narrower track going below power-line and pass small stone barn on right. Track now slightly wider and now rising gently. *This was almost certainly the old London Road before the new turnpike was built well to the east of Chipping Norton. We shall follow close to its course, through Old Chalford, Lidstone, Church Enstone and Cleveley and like to think that Shakespeare may also have done so, on his way to Oxford and London.* Where track bends slightly to right, turn right when Glyme Farm is visible over to left and immediately turn left to go over small waymarked stile.

(B) Go across field aiming for stile just to right of projecting hedge near modern barn. Good view of Glyme Farmhouse over to left. Over stile in electric fence and keep in same direction across field soon aiming for another stile, also in electric fence. Over this stile, keep in same direction to go over stile below large ash tree and cross wooden bridge over stream - this is our first encounter with the little River Glyme - the provider of water for several ornamental pools that we shall pass and the chief supplier for the great lake in Blenheim Park (see page 28). Veer slightly right to go across small field aiming for waymarked stile in hedge ahead. Over this stile and through thick hedge beyond, before veering right to follow well-defined path through the first of two plantations. Over stile at end of first plantation and across corner of field to go over stile into second plantation. Keep in same direction along path through this plantation and over stile at its end. Now veer to left to go along centre of field with ruins of stone barn in bushy area over to right. The little River Glyme is in valley below to right. Start to drop down field on slightly visible track aiming for large white notice-board beyond gate ahead. At end of field go over stile to left of large wooden gate and turn right onto track where sign for Glyme Valley Nature Reserve faces us.

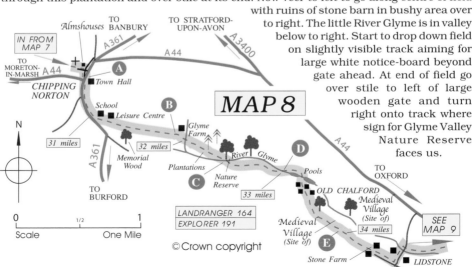

Market Street, Chipping Norton

(C) Go on track as it curves round to left and unobtrusively crosses the Glyme. Almost immediately fork left, off track and go through large metal gate into field, joining the Wychwood Way - *a 37-mile circular route around the heart of the former royal forest of Wychwood*. Now follow Wychwood Way waymarks until reaching the hamlet of Lidstone (see below). Keep along lower, left-hand edge of very long field with the Glyme on left in extensive woodlands - part of the Glyme Valley Nature Reserve. By coincidence we go onto a roughly-surfaced track where the woods on left come to an end. Just before end of field with large metal gate visible ahead, we bear left and go across the River Glyme at a ford. Go through large metal gate just beyond ford and after 10 paces turn right to follow well-defined path to go through another large metal gate. Keep across next field, climbing up bank on slightly visible path, still parallel with the Glyme, now below to right. Just beyond point where pool is visible down to right, go through small metal gate at end of field.

(D) Now turn right to go along and then up well-surfaced farm road beyond valley with attractive pools (with wildfowl) on both sides and park-like field on bank to left. Now keep on farm road, bearing up to left into large farmyard of Old Chalford Farm. Turn left in farmyard by two very large modern barns on right and go straight through farmyard with modern barns on right and old stone barns to left. Pass large brick-built barn on right and substantial farmhouse on left. Veer slightly left off track as it bends to right and go through gateway. Go diagonally right, across field aiming for middle and most distant power-pole. At end of field bear left onto track, through possible gateway and up slight slope. At top of rise veer right, off surfaced track and go through large metal gate. View of pool in valley down to left. Keep on track along top, right-hand edge of field. *Slight signs ahead, left, of earthworks of medieval Nether Chalford village.* Through large metal gate and keep in same direction along top side of field. Pass spring over to left with woodland just beyond.

(E) Through metal gate, crossing a not very apparent bridleway, and keep in same direction across next, smaller field. *Slight signs over to left, at top of bank across valley, of earthworks of Over Chalford. Both this and Nether Chalford (see above) were abandoned in about 1470, when they were given to Oriel College, Oxford, and cleared for highly profitable sheep grazing. Many medieval villages suffered a similar fate.* Through small metal gate and keep along left-hand edge of field with wooden fence to immediate left. At end of field go through farmyard of Stone Farm between two modern barns and onto surfaced farm road, ignoring bridleway sign to right. At far end of farm drive ignore gateway to right with waymark indicating Wychwood Way and we thus leave this particular route. Go straight ahead through gateway and immediately turn left with care onto public road to enter Lidstone hamlet.

Lane beyond Chipping Norton

(A) Go along public road and down steep little hill through attractive Lidstone hamlet. *Until the 1930s there used to be a small inn here, on the north side of the road. Called the Talbot Arms after the Talbots, the Earls of Shrewsbury of nearby Heythrop Park, it catered for travellers on the old road to London.* Pass disused chapel (*dated 1874*) on right, continue down road into valley and over bridge crossing little River Glyme. After about 20 paces beyond bridge turn right, off

Pool at Cleveley

road, through offset gap (SP *Church Enstone*) into wooded area and immediately cross boggy area on boardwalk. Go along well-defined, but possibly slippery, path through attractive woodland with River Glyme never far below to right and with bluebells much in evidence in late spring. Pass house with garden up to left, but possibly not visible in high summer. If in doubt go slightly up bank away from the Glyme, pass path coming in from left at inverted Y-junction. Over rudimentary stile in low wire cross-fence. Near end of woodland go up very slippery slope **with great care**. Beyond end of wood keep in same direction as the last few yards of woodland path, following waymark's direction to cut across corner of field. Soon aim for left-hand end of projecting wood. Note deer platform at edge of wood down to right. Bear right at outer corner of wood and follow to immediate left of its boundary. Where edge of wood again turns to right veer left following waymark's direction up across field on well-defined path.

(B) At end of field go over stone stile, **cross the busy A44 with great care**, go a few yards to right before going left to cross stone wall - either through gap or over stone stile. Now keep in same direction by going diagonally right through young, narrow plantation heading to immediate left of stone gate pillars. Cross surfaced farm drive to left of pillars and keep in same direction, going diagonally across field, heading for a not very obvious gap in cross-hedge ahead. Through this gap and keep in same direction across next field on well-defined path. Near end of field turn right to go over stile in low fence alongside before turning left to resume original line. Now head for low stone stile in wall ahead. *Church Enstone church tower visible in trees ahead left; Neat Enstone visible well over to right.* Over this stone stile and wooden stile just beyond. Keep in same direction across next field on well-defined path, soon starting to drop gently down. At end of field go through narrow gap in hedge (could be difficult to spot in high summer). Keep in almost the same direction down across next small field with wooden fence and house over to right. At end of fence on right go over high and awkward stile and down short, narrow pathway. Now turn right to go down short grassy swath to cross over surfaced entrance drive to Heythrop Park just to right of lodge and entrance gateway. Down possibly slippery path **with care** into wooded area, soon benefiting from a handrail for a short stretch. At bottom of grassy slope turn left onto surfaced roadway with old mill on left and cross River Glyme. Now up steep roadway into pretty village of Church Enstone and turn right at road junction by hospitable Crown Inn on left. (*But go straight ahead left if you wish to visit Enstone Church - visible from here. Dedicated to St Kenelm, the martyred boy-king of Mercia, this pleasing church has a fine Norman south doorway within its equally impressive 14th-century two-storeyed, vaulted porch. Do not miss the touching monument to Stevens Wisdom in the south aisle.*)

24

(C) Continue along road to junction with busier road and **with great care** go straight across this often busy B4030, onto roadway to immediate right of Rose Cottage. Soon turn left (SP - *Neat Enstone*) and go up curving track to immediate right of twin power-pole. At entrance gate to house called *The Barnslade*, turn left and immediately right to go along narrow path with wooden fence on right and wall on left. Over stile and turn left to go along top, left-hand edge of field. Over stile beside large metal gate and turn right with care to go down narrow, sunken, public road. At end of this narrow road **go with great care straight across often busy B4022** and onto grassy path to immediate left of hedge (SP - *Cleveley*). Go along this attractive grassy path with hedge on right and initially, a bank up to left. Eventually start to drop down into small valley with fence on left. Over wooden bridge crossing small tributary stream (could be dry in summer). Path now more muddy and less grassy. As we drop down towards Cleveley a waterfall, part of the mill sluice, visible over to right. Enter the attractive hamlet of Cleveley with large pool on left just beyond first house on left. *The old Chipping Norton-London road used to run through here and Shakespeare may well have passed this way. There were once two fulling mills here, one of which was converted to a cornmill, and was still working in the 1930s. All is now residential and very tranquil.*

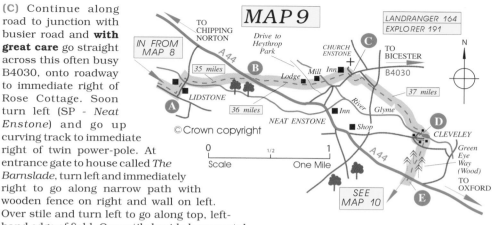

(D) Over bridge crossing the River Glyme with millhouse over to right - this is the last time we shall see the Glyme until reaching Woodstock, some 10 miles ahead, where it still performs a very valuable function. Turn left at road junction by small triangular green (SP - *Gagingwell*). After about 25 yards and **just before** passing House No 4 on right, turn right

up narrow pathway to immediate right of this house (SP - *Footpath*). Eventually emerge to cross public road by House No 2 on left and phone box on right and onto grassy track. At end of track veer slightly left and go along well-defined path in a long, narrow plantation known as The Green Eye Way.

(E) At end of plantation go through gap in hedge and **cross busy A44 with very great care** to go over low stone stile in gap in hedge (SP - *Fulwell*).

Summer afternoon at Cleveley

25

(A) Having **crossed busy A44 with very great care** to go over low stone stile in gap in hedge (SP - *Fulwell*), go straight across field on well-defined path initially aiming for power poles to right of wood well ahead. Soon drop down into small valley and in its bottom bear up left through wide gap in hedge into next field, keeping up its left-hand edge with hedge on immediate left. Go beneath two power lines and at end of field go onto track into woods. After about 25 paces turn left and almost immediately right to emerge from wood and keep on grassy track to left of this very large wood's left-hand edge - this is known as Deadman's Riding Wood. Pass reassuring waymark post, bluebells visible in wood in early summer. Follow track as it bends to left away from wood and towards a low stone barn. Soon bear right just before reaching barn and skirt around right-hand edge of barn and surrounding wall, bearing left and then finally right, as it leaves barn behind. Now keep along straight track with hedge to immediate left. *Ditchley Park (mansion) just visible at head of slope well over to right.*

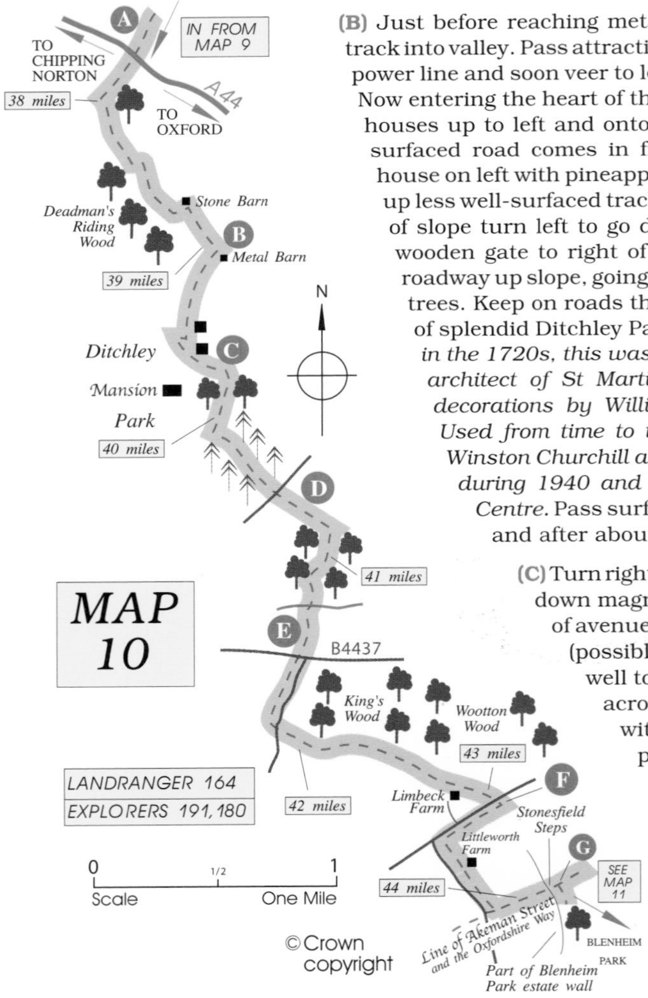

(B) Just before reaching metal barn turn right to go down track into valley. Pass attractive house over to right, go under power line and soon veer to left following track along valley. Now entering the heart of the Ditchley Park estate passing houses up to left and onto surfaced road where another surfaced road comes in from left. Immediately beyond house on left with pineapple-topped gate piers, turn right up less well-surfaced track. At T-junction of tracks at top of slope turn left to go down track and through small wooden gate to right of cattle-grid. Keep on surfaced roadway up slope, going over cross-roads beneath large trees. Keep on roads through parkland with glimpses of splendid Ditchley Park mansion over to right. *Built in the 1720s, this was designed by James Gibbs, the architect of St Martin's-in-the-Fields, with interior decorations by William Kent and Henry Flitcroft. Used from time to time as a weekend retreat by Winston Churchill and members of his War Cabinet during 1940 and 1941, it is now a Conference Centre.* Pass surfaced drive coming in from right and after about 50 paces - - -

(C) Turn right, off surfaced road to go straight down magnificent avenue of trees. At end of avenue go through large wooden gates (possibly use a small stile along fence well to right). Keep in same direction across narrower belt of parkland with many large trees to left. As parkland widens out look to right for excellent view of Ditchley Park's south front before bearing half-right and then turning left, to go down long, broad avenue between two belts of woodland. Look back from time to time as Ditchley's south front gradually sinks out of view like a great ship!

TO CHIPPING NORTON

38 miles

A44

IN FROM MAP 9

TO OXFORD

Deadman's Riding Wood

Stone Barn

39 miles

Metal Barn

N

Ditchley

Mansion

Park

40 miles

41 miles

MAP 10

B4437

King's Wood

Wootton Wood

43 miles

LANDRANGER 164
EXPLORERS 191, 180

42 miles

Limbeck Farm

Littleworth Farm

Stonesfield Steps

44 miles

SEE MAP 11

0   1/2   1
Scale   One Mile

© Crown copyright

Line of Akeman Street and the Oxfordshire Way

Part of Blenheim Park estate wall

BLENHEIM PARK

(D) At end of avenue go over stile to right of wooden gates and cross minor public road onto grassy bridleway track (SP - *Stonesfield*) with fields on both sides. Soon meet wood, now alongside on right. After about 300 yards of undulating track, where bridleways cross, turn right into woodland onto well-used bridleway. Keep on bridleway through initial belt of woodland soon veering left to go down the inside of the right-hand edge of wood. Bluebells here in early summer. Over wooden bridge crossing small stream and bear right to go along bridleway parallel with stream to right. Bear left, away from stream and up curving bridleway ignoring small wooden gate on right. Now keep on gradually ascending bridleway, partly overhung with bushes and small trees.

(E) At end of bridleway **go straight over the busy B4437 with great care** and down minor public road opposite (SP - *Stonesfield*). Keep down this road with care and after about 600 yards turn left through wide gap in hedge. Keep to immediate right of hedge (at right-angles to road) and path soon becomes grassy track. Follow track to corner of wood. Soon

The Stonesfield Steps at our entry to Blenheim Park

meet corner of wood (King's Wood) on left and keep to its immediate right along its southern edge. In places track becomes a narrow headland, but keep to it as it curves to left and later to right. Through very wide gap in cross-hedge still keeping to immediate right of wood (now Wootton Wood). Limbeck Farm visible ahead. Keep as close to edge of wood as possible when going across grass to left of Limbeck farmhouse. Through wide gateway into left-hand side of farmyard and keep in same direction with wood still on immediate left.

(F) At end of path, go through gap and turn right **with care to go along right-hand verge of busy minor road**. Pass drive to Limbeck Farm on right and after about 300 yards turn left at road junction (SP - *Combe*). Pass Littleworth Farm on left and after about 250 yards turn left through gap onto the Oxfordshire Way (*a 65-mile pathway running across Oxfordshire from Bourton-on-the-Water to Henley-on-Thames*) and the Wychwood Way (*see page 23*) to go along footpath to immediate left of sporadic hedge. *We are now following the course of the Romans' Akeman Street, but there are no obvious signs of it here. Akeman Street was an important Roman road running from Cirencester to Bicester and on to St Albans. (Please note that from here until reaching Woodstock our route follows rights-of-way (but with no waymarks) through Blenheim Park, entry to which is normally charged. If you wish to stray from the right-of-way, you must enter the park through the entrance gate in Woodstock referred to on page 29 and pay the required entry fee.)* Go up wooden steps, known as the Stonesfield Steps, to cross the massive dry-stone estate wall of Blenheim Park. *No less than nine miles in length, this was built in 1729, about 25 years after the great park, previously the royal hunting preserve of Woodstock Manor, was given by the Crown to John Churchill, 1st Duke of Marlborough.*

(G) After 30 paces turn right at crossing of tracks leaving Akeman Street, the Oxfordshire Way and the Wychwood Way and go along track through woodlands.

(A) After 200 yards turn left to go along grassy path and over wooden bridge over often dry stream-bed. Soon turn right at edge of woodlands and follow their left-hand edge for about 50 paces before going across large field on grassy track, still keeping in same direction. At far edge of field bear left by waymark post to join track with a wood to immediate right. At end of track turn right onto surfaced roadway and after about 60 paces turn left to go over stile in wooden fence. Go across long, narrow field to go over second stile, also in wooden fence. Now veer right initially aiming for left-hand edge of right-hand of two circular plantations of copper-beech trees (*but only one plantation visible in summer*). Soon head for stile in cross-fence to left of spinney. The great Column of Victory, the focal point of Blenheim Park, now visible ahead left. Over stile in cross-fence and turn right to follow to immediate left of fence, then skirt around to immediate left of plantation and follow to immediate left of fence beyond, keeping in same direction.

(B) At end of field go over stile beneath horse-chestnut tree and turn left onto estate road by entry to Park Farm's farmyard on right. Almost immediately bear right and then left keeping on estate road, with glimpses of Park Farm's farmhouse to right. After about 500 yards bear left at inverted Y-junction of estate roads by triangular 'green' with three large trees. After about 300 yards, at bottom of slope, turn left over stile in electric fence and go beneath horse-chestnut tree heading for right-hand fence corner just ahead. Bear left at this fence corner and follow to its immediate right aiming just to the right of the Column of Victory. At end of fence keep in same direction passing just to the right of the Column of Victory (following the right-of-way). *When passing the Column, spend time to look left, up to it and to the Ditchley Gate Lodge, well over a mile beyond to the north-west. But, more significantly look down to the right, beyond the Grand Bridge to the spectacle of Blenheim Palace's north front. Vanbrugh's palace design is magnificent, perhaps a little overwhelming, but the splendid 2500-acre park through which we are walking, absorbs it effortlessly. The landscaping of the park is largely the work of Capability Brown and his damming of the little River Glyme provided a great lake worthy of Vanbrugh's massive bridge spanning it.* Now veer right with views of lake ahead, right. Gradually drop down slope, heading for three cedar trees below and go over stile in electric fence just beyond.

(C) Beyond stile, turn left onto estate road. After about 130 paces turn right to go down across grass to immediate left of wooden fence, with cottage beyond it. Now turn right onto another estate road. *Splendid views of lake down to right with Blenheim Palace well over to right, beyond it.* Just before reaching stone bridge over the River Glyme turn left to go through wooden door beside large, solid wooden gate in estate wall and turn right to go

through second gate (make sure you shut both), effectively entering town of Woodstock. Now turn right to go **with care** along narrow pavement to immediate right of the busy A44. Go on sunken path passing row of cottages on right and bend to left up hill on very narrow pavement. Soon turn right into Hoggrove Hill, up flower-bordered and stepped path. At top of path keep in same direction to go along small street known as Chaucer's Lane.

Lake shore in Blenheim Park

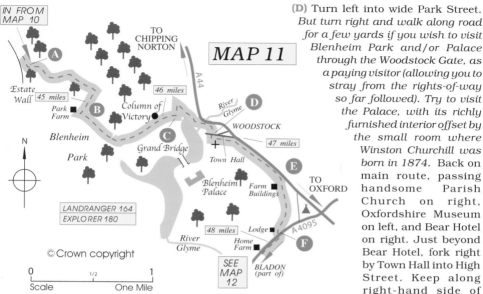

MAP 11

IN FROM MAP 10

TO CHIPPING NORTON

Estate Wall — 45 miles

Park Farm — 46 miles

Column of Victory

Blenheim

Park

Grand Bridge

LANDRANGER 164
EXPLORER 180

© Crown copyright

N

0   1/2   1
Scale   One Mile

River Glyme

WOODSTOCK

47 miles

Town Hall

Blenheim Palace

Farm Buildings

TO OXFORD

A4095

48 miles   Lodge

River Glyme

Home Farm

SEE MAP 12

BLADON (part of)

(D) Turn left into wide Park Street. *But turn right and walk along road for a few yards if you wish to visit Blenheim Park and/or Palace through the Woodstock Gate, as a paying visitor (allowing you to stray from the rights-of-way so far followed). Try to visit the Palace, with its richly furnished interior offset by the small room where Winston Churchill was born in 1874.* Back on main route, passing handsome Parish Church on right, Oxfordshire Museum on left, and Bear Hotel on right. Just beyond Bear Hotel, fork right by Town Hall into High Street. Keep along right-hand side of eventually widening High Street, passing many shops, restaurants and inns. *Do spend time looking round Woodstock - a most pleasant town.* At end of High Street, by Millennium Stone on left, bear right with care onto A44, Oxford Street, still keeping to pavement on right-hand side of road. Now leaving Woodstock, passing garage on left and another very impressive entrance to Blenheim Park and Palace on right.

(E) After about half-a-mile, and just beyond a de-restriction sign and a stone 'Welcome to Woodstock' feature on right, turn right to go through gap in low wall and down short, narrow pathway (SP - *Bladon*). Over stile and bear slightly left and then right to go along field parallel with high stone estate wall to right and caravan park well over to left. Pass office in converted farm buildings beyond wall on right and cross access road. Bear right near end of wall by large ash tree and head for stile below horse-chestnut tree. Go over this stile and through small wooden gate just beyond.

(F) Cross minor estate road at minor entry to Blenheim Park by small lodge on right. Go along path at our entry to the long stretched-out village of Bladon with stone wall to immediate right and grass to left and soon **cross busy A4095 with great care**. Keep in same direction down left-hand pavement beside A4095. Ignore footpath sign to left and eventually pass Home Farm on right.

House at Woodstock

29

(A) Opposite the White House Inn, Bladon, on right, turn left off A4095 up small road between wooden fences (SP - *Church*). Turn right through small metal gate into Bladon churchyard to head for tower at west end of church. *Just before reaching this, pass on left, the simple tombstone of Sir Winston and Lady Clementine Churchill, and also those of Sir Winston's father, Randolph, and Sir Winston's son, Randolph, together with those of several other members of his family. Pause here awhile to reflect on the miracles achieved by our threatened nation under his inspired leadership, in the darkest days of the 39-45 War. When I last came here someone had left a small posy of flowers at the foot of Sir Winston's tomb with a card simply inscribed -* **"Our Greatest Ever - How we need you now"**. Now go straight on, passing the west doorway beneath the tower and leaving the churchyard by its lychgate, *having perhaps visited the small Churchill Exhibition inside the church.* Keep straight along Church Street and keep on it across intersection of roads at `The Green`, passing bench and noticeboard on left and Rectory Farm, just beyond. At small cross-roads bear left, up Heath Lane. Pass another noticeboard on right. At end of Heath Lane go ahead, up concrete roadway with garages to left and go through small metal gate beside large one (SP - *Begbroke*). Keep along left-hand side of field with hedge on immediate left.

(B) Veer right near end of field and then veer left to go through small wooden gate into extensive woodlands of Bladon Heath. Follow grassy track through beautiful broadleaf woodlands. Ignore track up to right and go over wooden bridge crossing not too apparent stream. At one or two points it may be necessary to veer off track to avoid boggy patches. Emerge from woods through small wooden gate and go along left-hand edge of field with hedge to immediate left, aim for dutch barn well ahead. Ignore two hedge gaps to left and veer right to continue along left-hand edge of field. At far end of field go through small wooden gate and along narrow path between hedge on left and garden fence on right. Go quietly here as path is very close to house with attractive garden.

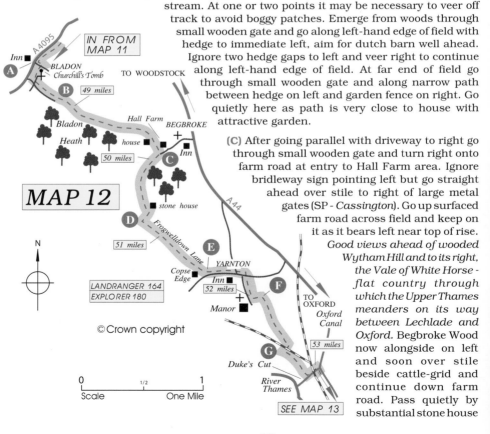

(C) After going parallel with driveway to right go through small wooden gate and turn right onto farm road at entry to Hall Farm area. Ignore bridleway sign pointing left but go straight ahead over stile to right of large metal gates (SP - *Cassington*). Go up surfaced farm road across field and keep on it as it bears left near top of rise. *Good views ahead of wooded Wytham Hill and to its right, the Vale of White Horse - flat country through which the Upper Thames meanders on its way between Lechlade and Oxford.* Begbroke Wood now alongside on left and soon over stile beside cattle-grid and continue down farm road. Pass quietly by substantial stone house

30

on left and just beyond, turn right at cross-roads of tracks to go along track towards wide gap in hedge.

(D) Go through this wide gap in hedge and turn left to go along track with hedge to immediate left. Good view of Cassington's church spire in middle-distance, down to right. Where track turns to right, go straight ahead onto an initially wide 'green road', known as Frogwelldown Lane, with hedges on both sides. Green road soon obscured and becomes a narrow path through bushes, although still following its previous line. *Expect to have low-flying aircraft in this area as*

Tombstone of Sir Winston and Lady Clementine Churchill at Bladon

we are now beneath one of Oxford Airport's approaches. Path soon starts a long and gradual descent and finally emerges onto a roughly-surfaced track at the entry to Yarnton.

(E) Pass house called Copse Edge on right before bearing left onto minor public road into Yarnton using pavement on right-hand side of road. Pass Red Lion Inn on right and ignore footpath sign to right. Pass phone box on right. Go straight, not left, at road junction in centre of Yarnton (SP - *Kidlington*) and after about 50 paces, turn right onto quieter road (SP - *St Bartholomew's Church*). Pass house called *The Old School* on right. Opposite second gate to church on right and Yarnton Manor gateway just beyond, turn left off road to go over stile beside large wooden gate. *But do not miss a visit to Yarnton Church. This has a medieval cross-shaft near its south door, and within its unspoilt interior, a unique series of early stained glass windows. Even more appealing are the splendid monuments to various members of the Spencer family, whose distant forbears, like Shakespeare's, came from Snitterfield, near Stratford-upon-Avon.* After visiting the church, go over stile opposite and along left-hand edge of field with fence on immediate left

(F) At end of field go over stile and immediately fork right to go diagonally across field following direction of right-hand waymark on stile. *Between here and Duke's Cut (end of Para G), waymarking may not be too frequent and you are advised to follow route directions below with great care.* Soon aim for stile just to right of far corner of field. Go under high-voltage power-line before crossing stile. Now go along left-hand edge of next field with hedge and trees on immediate left. At far left-hand corner of field go over stile in cross-fence and keep in same direction across next field with sporadic hedge and trees to left. *All signs of dismantled branch railway have gone, although it may show on your edition of the OS Explorer Map.* Over wooden bridge crossing stream with main railway embankment now to our right. Now keep along right-hand edge of field with hedge to immediate right and railway embankment just visible beyond.

(G) Before reaching end of field turn right through metal gate and go through underbridge beneath railway embankment. Turn left after emerging from underbridge and follow left-hand edge of field veering slightly away from railway embankment. Just before end of field turn left through large gap in hedge and over not very apparent bridge before turning right to follow right-hand edge of next field. Go through not very obvious gap in thick hedge about 15 paces to left of field corner and emerge into next field. Veer left to go diagonally across field and near its end, bear right onto short, grassy track between two wire fences. Soon veer left and through small gateway. Now heading along towpath of Duke's Cut (a branch of the Oxford Canal, linking it with the Thames).

(A) Use towpath to pass Duke's Cut Lock going below railway bridge and turn right to cross mellow-brick bridge and go along surfaced towpath beside the Oxford Canal. Under massive bridges beneath the noisy A40 and the even noisier A34 (Oxford Bypass). Soon pass possible permanently moored narrow-boats, some of which look a little tired, and then pass Canal Bridge No 234.

(B) At Wolvercote Lock, with picnic tables on its right, turn right up stepped path and turn right at top to go along right-hand side of busy public road immediately crossing railway bridge. *(But it is possible to go into Oxford more directly, but less pleasantly, by continuing along towpath for two and a half miles, to re-join the main route at Point E.)* Having crossed railway bridge go down road towards Wolvercote village, crossing to left-hand side of road as soon as possible. Views over to left of the great Port Meadow, which stretches well over a mile southwards from here. Enter Wolvercote and follow road through village keeping along left-hand pavement. Turn left by White Hart Inn and Red Lion Inn and almost immediately bear round to right, still beside road. Pass car park, riverside picnic site and toilets on left. Over bridge crossing branch of River Thames, pass Trout Inn on left and two further branches of River Thames.

(C) Turn left through small wooden gate just beyond second bridge over River Thames, joining the Thames Path. *This is a well-used National Trail following the Thames from its source near Cirencester to the Thames Barrier below Greenwich - a total distance of 180 miles. Initially we shall follow it for about two miles until reaching Oxford.* Keep along surfaced path passing to immediate left of ruins of Godstow Abbey. *This was founded in 1139 and Rosamund de Clifford, mistress of Henry II, was buried here, after her mysterious death.* Pass Godstow Lock, which like all Thames locks, is operated by a keeper, rather than by boat crews as is the case with most waterways. Along pleasant path with the River Thames never far away to left and the great expanse of Port Meadow beyond it. Good view of wooded Wytham Hill well over to right. As we get nearer to Oxford, some of its 'dreaming spires' become visible, but today these are unfortunately punctuated with tall modern buildings and usually a few cranes - such is progress! Through small wooden gate and pass pathway leading right to the Perch Inn, Binsey, a short distance away. Keep ahead here and well beyond, fork left at Y-junction of paths to keep close to river. Through metal gate and keep on track passing to left of Bossom's Boatyard. Fork left as soon as possible to keep close to river.

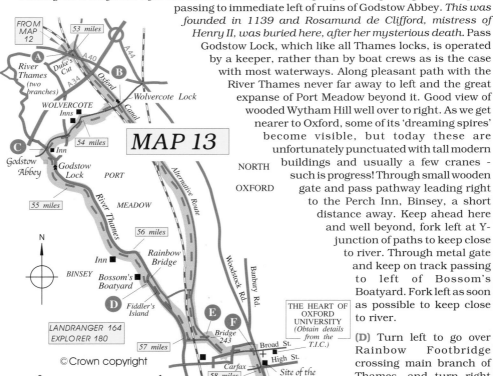

(D) Turn left to go over Rainbow Footbridge crossing main branch of Thames, and turn right keeping on Thames Path.

Now go along left-hand side of Thames and at end of marina down to left, go straight ahead ignoring footbridge to left and going over a footbridge ahead. Now go along pleasant tree-shaded path on right bank of long Fiddlers' Island, still with main branch of Thames to immediate right. Pass three benches beside path as it bends to left. Leave Thames Path, ignoring footbridge to right and go straight ahead (SP - *Oxford Canal*) keeping to left of small feeder canal linking the Thames to the Oxford Canal. Under series of very low railway bridges (**watch your head!**), then veer left and then right on narrow path, with remains of old railway swing-bridge over to right. Emerge into manicured area with flats to left and go over paved roadway onto tarmac path curving round to left. Pass Snakes' Island Nature Conservation Area on right with canal link just beyond it.

(**E**) Over footbridge crossing branch of Thames and turn very sharp right to go over elegant Canal Bridge No 243. (*We are joined here by our Oxford Canal Alternative Path which started at Wolvercote Lock (Point **B**), some two and a half miles to the north.*) Continue beyond bridge on towpath to right of canal, beyond Isis Lock, the navigational linking point with the Thames. Enter urban Oxford at end of the Oxford Canal, which used to go beyond this point to busy wharves, the site of which is now occupied by Nuffield College. Turn left onto busy Hythe Bridge Street (SP - *Gloucester Green*) with the Hythe Bridge just down to right. **You will take some minutes to get used to busy traffic conditions, so go over cross-roads by pedestrian crossing with very great care** (SP - *Gloucester Green*) and go straight up right-hand side of George Street. Pass Odeon Cinema and New Theatre, both on left.

(**F**) At top of George Street, turn right at cross-roads into pedestrianised road known as the Cornmarket (*but go straight over into Broad Street if you wish to explore more of Oxford - No space here to describe it, but there is a helpful Tourist Information Centre on Broad Street's right-hand side and several splendid bookshops close by!*). Go along left-hand side of Cornmarket, passing the Church of St Michael at the Northgate on left, with its Saxon tower. Pass entry to Golden Cross Shopping Centre on left and after 20 paces pass Republic Clothing shop (No 3) on left, with a staircase beside leading to a betting shop and beyond it on the 2nd floor to the modest offices of an organisation known as Oxford Aunts. *Here, in Shakespeare's time, was the Crown Tavern, which was owned by John Davenant and his attractive wife, who were friends of the poet and it is reasonably certain that he stayed here on his journeys between Stratford and London. (For further details see pages 76-77.) As recently as 1927 very early wallpaper was discovered in one of the tavern's rooms and since then it has been known as the* Painted Room. *This is full of atmosphere and interest and is a world away from the bustle in the street and shops below. The wallpaper is well preserved*

behind a sliding panel and there is an engraved portrait of Sir William Davenant, John's son and Shakespeare's godson. If you wish to visit the Painted Room (only possible on Monday - Friday) it will be necessary to give notice by telephoning 01865 791017. Arrive at Carfax, the centre of Oxford, with the tower of St Martin's church over to right. Go straight across into St Aldate's Street to start Chapter 3. (**But turn left down High Street, if you wish to explore more of Oxford.**)

The Thames from Wolvercote Bridge with ruins of Godstow Abbey in the background

Chapter 3   Oxford to Marlow

(A) From Carfax, the centre of the city of Oxford, go straight across, southwards, down St Aldate's Street. Pass Museum of Oxford on left, Post Office on right, St Aldate's Church on right, Pembroke College, up to right and Christ Church on left, with its splendid Tom Tower, the work of Christopher Wren. Pass entry to Christ Church Gardens and Christ Church Meadows on left, and opposite, on right, *Alice's Shop,* reminding us that Charles Dodgson, the writer of *Alice in Wonderland,* was a maths tutor at Christ Church and that Alice Liddell, the inspiration for his books, was the daughter of its Dean. At road junction go straight ahead, keeping on St Aldate's and passing Police Station on left. Pass Head of the River Inn on left and over Folly Bridge crossing the Thames. Pass

Tom Tower, Christ Church

Salter's Steamers Ltd on left and an eccentric, castellated Victorian house on right. This is called *The Folly* and was inspired by memories of a curious building known as *Friar Bacon's Folly,* which once stood here and which was used by the Friar as an observatory.

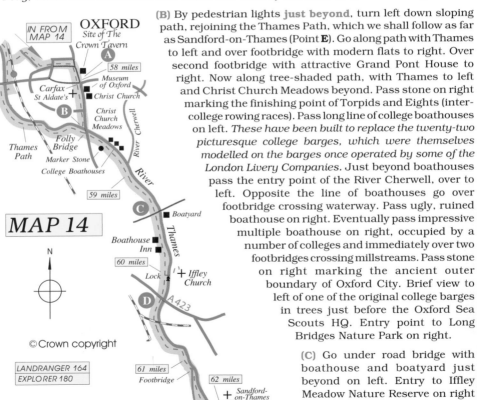

(B) By pedestrian lights **just beyond**, turn left down sloping path, rejoining the Thames Path, which we shall follow as far as Sandford-on-Thames (Point **E**). Go along path with Thames to left and over footbridge with modern flats to right. Over second footbridge with attractive Grand Pont House to right. Now along tree-shaded path, with Thames to left and Christ Church Meadows beyond. Pass stone on right marking the finishing point of Torpids and Eights (inter-college rowing races). Pass long line of college boathouses on left. *These have been built to replace the twenty-two picturesque college barges, which were themselves modelled on the barges once operated by some of the London Livery Companies.* Just beyond boathouses pass the entry point of the River Cherwell, over to left. Opposite the line of boathouses go over footbridge crossing waterway. Pass ugly, ruined boathouse on right. Eventually pass impressive multiple boathouse on right, occupied by a number of colleges and immediately over two footbridges crossing millstreams. Pass stone on right marking the ancient outer boundary of Oxford City. Brief view to left of one of the original college barges in trees just before the Oxford Sea Scouts HQ. Entry point to Long Bridges Nature Park on right.

(C) Go under road bridge with boathouse and boatyard just beyond on left. Entry to Iffley Meadow Nature Reserve on right and pass several benches on right. Pass Oxford Brookes University Boathouse on right and, not far beyond, the Isis Tavern on right.

Map labels (Map 14):
IN FROM MAP 14
OXFORD
Site of The Crown Tavern
A
58 miles
Museum of Oxford
Carfax
St Aldate's
Christ Church
B
Christ Church Meadows
River Cherwell
Folly Bridge
Thames Path
Marker Stone
College Boathouses
59 miles
River Thames
MAP 14
N
C
Boatyard
Boathouse Inn
60 miles
Lock
D
Iffley Church
A423
© Crown copyright
LANDRANGER 164
EXPLORER 180
0   1/2   1
Scale   One Mile
61 miles
Footbridge
62 miles
Sandford-on-Thames
E
Lock   Inn
SEE MAP 17

Good view of Iffley's church tower rising amongst trees beyond Iffley Lock. Pass to right of Iffley Lock area. (*But walk to left if you wish to visit Iffley Church, with its fine Norman features, including two chancel arches. Turn left to cross lower lock gates and leave lock area by crossing two footbridges and onto narrow path. Follow road as it curves uphill, turn right at its top and go along road to arrive at church on right.*) Back on main route, having kept to the right of Iffley Lock area, leave it through small wooden gate. Keep on path beside Thames, with Iffley Meadow Nature Reserve still on right. Pass a very welcome memorial seat on right and - - -

Oxford College Boathouses

(D) Go under very large road bridge carrying A423, Oxford's Southern Bypass. Keep along path overhung with tall and beautiful trees. Over long footbridge crossing the Hinksey Stream where it empties into the Thames. Immediately fork left under railway bridge and through kissing gate into large meadow. Keep along meadow with Thames just to left and large electricity pylons to right. Pass large stone with metal plaque on its far side commemorating the Oxford Preservation Trust's acquisition of the meadow. Pass handsome early 19th-century house on far bank of Thames and veer slightly right where Thames bends away to left. Now follow well defined path across open space, cutting off bending Thames. Where path re-joins Thames go through gap beneath trees and follow path with bushes to right and river to left, soon turning left to go over substantial steel footbridge crossing branch of Thames and go briefly between the two branches. Pass one of the old college barges moored on edge of park-like garden over to left. Over two wooden bridges crossing waterways, the second of which is above a weir, and through small wooden gate just beyond. Sandford Lock now visible ahead as we cross an open meadow.

(E) Through gate into Sandford Lock area and go to far end of lock before turning left to go over lower lock gates. Continue over the millstream bridge, turn left alongside the King's Arms and head into outdoor eating area. Follow path round to right and go out into car park. Cross car park and turn left onto public road into Sandford-on-Thames village. Keep on road as it curves uphill and soon passes Sandford Church on left. Its attractive 17th-century porch was donated by Eliza Isham, and is delightfully inscribed, *Thanks to thy charitie religious dame, which found me old and made me new againe.*

Norman doorway, Iffley Church

(A) Bear right with care beyond Sandford-on-Thames Church onto busier road passing the Catherine Wheel Inn on right. Cross to left-hand side of road and soon turn left at road junction down Brick Kiln Lane (SP - *Reading*). Keep on left-hand pathway beside busy road, going beneath concrete road bridge. Keep on pathway as it veers slightly left, away from road. As main path bends round to left, turn right to go along short path **before crossing two busy roads to immediate right of roundabout with very great care - look right at first crossing and look left at second one.** After road crossing go up surfaced footpath (SP - *Garsington*) with hedges on both sides. Soon continue in same direction along quiet roadway and passing two entrances to estate of trim mobile homes.

(B) Beyond estate go along narrower roadway and when meeting metal gate across it, turn right to go along path to immediate right of metal sewage works fence. At outer corner of metal fence turn left and follow to its immediate right, with sporadic wire fence on right. After about 300 yards follow path as it veers slightly right away from sewage works fence to follow partly-surfaced path into more open area. Keep down field in approximately the same direction on now well-surfaced path. Many signs of suburban Oxford over to left. At end of path keep in same direction down roughly-surfaced track. Where track veers to right go through possibly gated gap and turn right onto surfaced path running parallel with busy road up to left.

(C) After about 250 yards veer right to go over stile and sleeper bridge. After thirty paces go over second stile, cross concrete roadway and over third stile. Go up right-hand edge of field with hedge on immediate right, soon passing part of Sandfordbrake Farm on right and leaving suburban south Oxford at last. *Distant line of the Chilterns visible ahead left.* At end of field veer very slightly left to go through gap and over sleeper bridge. Keep in same direction across next field aiming for right-hand side of wide gap between two wooded areas on slope ahead. Follow path as it gently rises towards end of field and at its end veer slightly left to go up quite steep grassy track through wide gap. Go along left-hand edge of field with hedge and trees to immediate left.

(D) Well before meeting high-voltage power-lines, at a slight dip in field, turn left below last willow tree on left to go over two stiles in thick hedge. Go diagonally right up across next field cutting off top right-hand corner. Go beneath high-voltage power-line and soon veer left to go along top right-hand edge of field with hedge to immediate right. Through gap in cross-fence and at end of second field keep in same direction, joining roughly-surfaced track with sporadic hedge on right and fence on left. Where track veers to right continue ahead over stile beside metal gate and go between hedge on right and fence and bushes on left. Turn right by metal gates to left and up mown grassy sward with shrubs on right and garden fences on left thereby entering Toot Baldon. Keep in same direction joining roughly-surfaced roadway.

Our path towards Toot Baldon

(E) Turn left with care onto minor public road. Ignore road to left to Wilmot's (housing estate) and keep along public road. Turn right at road junction just before reaching the Mole Inn and go down surfaced drive below fine avenue of horse-chestnut trees. *Fine views over to left of the long line of the Chilterns, our next significant destination.* Pass tennis court, garden and large house (*Court Leys*) on left and pass St Lawrence's Church just beyond. *This was heavily restored in the 19th century but retains some interesting details, especially the north-arcade capitals. In the churchyard there is the base of a 15th-century cross and a*

View from Toot Baldon Churchyard

welcome bench with lovely views southwards to the Chilterns across a valley below. Bear right by lychgate, go to right of new cemetery and along grassy terrace path.

(F) Go through wooden kissing gate and straight ahead down track to immediate right of house with postbox in its wall. Pass sign to Yew Tree Cottage on right and keep straight up track, passing door of Chapel Cottage and turning to right, following narrow grassy path around its rear. Through small wooden gate and go diagonally across right-hand corner of field aiming for right-hand end of small and low brick-built barn. Through kissing gate to right of barn and along very short grassy track before turning left onto public road at entry to Marsh Baldon. Pass Perry Cottage on left and between large barns of Parsonage Farm.

(G) Bear round to right and then immediately left opposite Parsonage Farm keeping on public road. Pass *Willowbrook* (house) on right and soon turn left onto surfaced track (SP - *Bridleway*). Keep straight ahead passing bridleway tracks to left and right and continue on towards farm buildings ahead. Go right, then left, through famyard with dutch barns.

Continue down track resuming approximately the same (eastward) direction. Pleasant open country ahead. After about 300 yards, where hedge and ditch come in from right, look out for remains of wooden gate on right with waymark. Go diagonally right here, to cross very large field, initially aiming for forked oak tree. On reaching vicinity of oak tree, veer left to cross next section of field approximately eastwards.

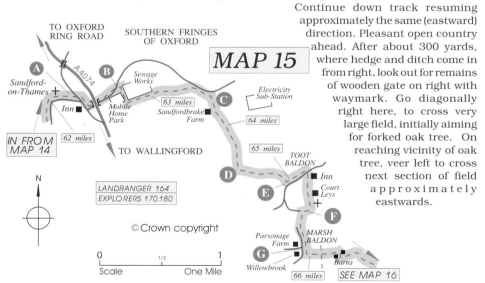

TO OXFORD RING ROAD

SOUTHERN FRINGES OF OXFORD

MAP 15

A

B

Sandford-on-Thames

A4074

Sewage Works

Inn

Mobile Home Park

63 miles

Sandfordbrake Farm

Electricity Sub-Station

C

64 miles

IN FROM MAP 14

62 miles

TO WALLINGFORD

65 miles

TOOT BALDON

D

Inn

Court Leys

E

F

N

LANDRANGER 164
EXPLORERS 170.180

©Crown copyright

0   1/2   1
Scale   One Mile

Parsonage Farm

MARSH BALDON

G

Willowbrook

66 miles

Barns

SEE MAP 16

(A) At end of field go over substantial footbridge crossing ditch and veer slightly right to go up next field on (hopefully) well-defined path. At end of field go over stile beneath oak tree and keep along left-hand edge of next field below oak trees with hedge to immediate left. Through wide gap in cross-hedge and keep along left-hand edge of next field. *Tree-capped Wittenham Clumps visible well over to right - these overlook the winding River Thames.* Over

sleeper bridge in wide gap in cross-hedge and keep along left-hand edge of next field. Near end of field bear right and after 55 paces turn left through gap in hedge to cross wooden bridge. Go diagonally across next very large field on (hopefully) well-defined path, initially aiming just to left of low-voltage power-pole in front of poplar trees and then veering a little to left. Over small bridge beneath oak tree, through small oak plantation and soon turn right onto grassy track.

The River Thame from Chiselhampton Bridge

(B) Soon turn left with care onto busy B4015, crossing to far (right-hand) side of road to use verge. Enter Chiselhampton, passing modern bungalows on left and soon **keep on right-hand verge down narrow length of road, with very great care.** Turn right onto even busier B480 by the Coach and Horses Inn ahead (SP - *Watlington*) and after a few yards **cross with great care to opposite side of road by bus stop.** Now use pavement on this, the left-hand side of B480. Leave Chiselhampton and go over bridge crossing River Thame. Keep on pavement beside busy road and after bearing left around a long bend, about 500 yards beyond bridge, turn left to go over double stile in tall willow hedge opposite signs on road and on post, stating SLOW, to vehicles coming towards us. Go diagonally right across narrow strip of meadow and go over wooden footbridge crossing stream and ignoring footpath to right. Go straight across next strip of meadow aiming for two hawthorn trees. Turn right to go between hawthorn trees and follow up wide grassy sward towards gate and kissing gate. Bear left and then right at end of sward and over stile to go along pleasant grassy track. Stadhampton's church tower soon visible ahead. Pass school playing fields and school on right.

(C) Over stile beside metal gate and turn right onto surfaced road at our entry to Stadhampton.

IN FROM MAP 15

MAP 16

67 miles

A
Footbridge
N
B4015
B
68 miles
River Thame

LANDRANGER 164
EXPLORERS 170,171

+ CHISELHAMPTON
A329
Inn
C
+ STADHAMPTON
TO THAME
D
Inn
B480
70 miles
69 miles
Footbridge
Granary & Dovecote
Ascott Farm
E
71 miles
TO WALLINGFORD

0   1/2   1
Scale   One Mile

© Crown copyright

Brook Surgery

SEE MAP 17

38

Stadhampton Church

Enter wide village green with gate to churchyard well over to left by noticeboard. *The church has an attractive 18th-century tower with finials at its corners but the rest was re-built in 1875 and is not of outstanding interest to visitors.* At end of road **cross busy A329 with great care** and go along minor road opposite, aiming towards attractive old stone house at far side of green. But just before reaching this house with its pond, bear right to follow surfaced road. On reaching first cottage on right (*The Lime House*) bear left through metal kissing gate leaving Cat Lane. Follow winding path through bushy area and over stile into field. Go across field on well-defined grassy path (**beware of possible holes**) soon ignoring path going diagonally left just beyond bushes on left. At end of field go across path running at right-angles along narrow belt of woodland and go over rudimentary stile into field. Go along right-hand edge of field with fence and avenue of trees to immediate right. On meeting another avenue running at right-angles to our route, turn right through gateway in fence (possibly not waymarked) and immediately turn left to continue in same direction, but now along left-hand edge of this, next field. *Note two pleasant old buildings over to right, one a granary and one a dovecote. These two buildings together with the avenues of trees and three stone gateways (not visible from our route) are all that remain of Ascott Park, a mansion ambitiously rebuilt in about 1660 but sadly burnt down before it was even completed.*

At end of field go over stile between metal gates and go across left-hand edge of farmyard with barns to immediate left. Through metal gate and bear left to join surfaced roadway. Note attractive pool over to right.

(**D**) Soon turn sharp right at road junction (SP - *Chalgrove*) and after about 120 paces, turn left to go through metal gate. Go straight across farmyard of Ascott Farm keeping to immediate left of barns and through or over large metal gates. Veer slightly right and go across short field heading for easily spotted stile in cross-fence. Over stile and veer slightly right approaching fence-line to right obliquely and initially aiming just to the right of a prominent landmark (a radio mast) on the Chiltern ridge well ahead (but **not** the Post Office Tower, which is very far to left). Over easily missed small stile in fence and keep in same direction across next field aiming to right-hand end of bushy area projecting from left-hand end of field.

Old granary at Ascott Park

(**E**) At end of field go over footbridge and stile just beyond and cross short section of rough grass. Now go across large field aiming for small building just visible through gap in hedge and trees well ahead (this might be obscured in later years). Cross track into next field (no fences or hedges here) and keep in same direction still aiming for small red-roofed building and going roughly parallel with road some 30 yards over to our left. Near end of field veer left, now aiming for larger building with low pitched roof beyond trimmed hedge. Aim for centre of trimmed hedge and at end of field go over stile in trimmed hedge. Now go through allotments on grassy path and at its end go over stile and turn left to cross car park of Brook Surgery.

(A) After 20 paces turn right onto public road and keep on pavement on right-hand side of road to enter Chalgrove and walk right through village on its High Street. (*You may find the next mile or so boring but you will pass useful shops and no fewer than three inns!*) Pass Lamb Inn on right and 'Beware Ducks' sign on left. Stream now along left-hand side of road. Pass garage on right, useful shops on right (including general store and pharmacy), John Hampden (Village) Hall on left, Post Office and Village Store on left. *John Hampden, brave*

Parliamentarian leader, died in June 1643 as a result of injuries received at the Battle of Chalgrove Field, just to the north of the village. Pass Crown Inn on right, Red Lion Inn on left and War Memorial on right. Pass school on right and phone box on right. Pass turn to church on right. *The Church of St Mary is a substantial building with an unspoilt interior which contains, among other things, an outstanding series of medieval wall paintings. It will probably be locked but there is a list of keyholders beside the north door.* Pass attractive thatched cottages on right. Where road bends round to left, bear right on to Berrick Road (SP - *Berrick Salome*) and leave Chalgrove.

(B) Beyond last bungalow on right and immediately beyond bridge with white-painted railings, turn left to go over stile (SP - *Brightwell Baldwin*). Go along left-hand edge of small triangular field. Immediately beyond power-pole, veer slightly right to go over stile in tall hedge and turn left to go along surfaced road. Keep on road through woodlands in valley and emerge by concrete apron on right. After another 120 paces on surfaced road turn left onto short, roughly-surfaced track between willow trees.

Cottage at Chalgrove

After 20 paces fork right, off track (SP *Footpath*) and go along narrow path in largely ash plantation. At end of path turn right through gap and veer left to go along well-defined path across field. Attractive Cadwell Farmhouse visible over to right. Up gentle rise initially aiming for gap in trees on skyline ahead.

(C) At end of field cross track and go over stile into woodlands. Go straight along cleared ride in woodlands with large Cedar of Lebanon visible far ahead. Over stile beside wooden gate at end of woodlands and keep in same direction across short field with large walled garden visible over to right. Through kissing gate into next field, now attractive parkland, still aiming for Cedar of Lebanon. Remaining wing of Brightwell Park (*mansion demolished*) visible up to right and interesting 17th-century dovecote shaped as a Greek cross visible down to left. Go through kissing gate just to left of massive Cedar of Lebanon and veer down left to go to immediate right of low horse-jumps and then veer right through small group of horse-chestnut trees.

(D) Now go over stile beside small wooden gate and turn left with care onto public road. (But turn right to enter village of Brightwell Baldwin, with the pretty, flower-decked Lord Nelson Inn on the left after 100 yards and the Church of St Bartholomew opposite. *This sits above a sloping churchyard and has a pleasantly atmospheric interior with 18th-century pews, a Jacobean pulpit with tester, and some handsome monuments, especially one vast one, in the north aisle chapel to members of the Stone and Lowe families. There is also much interesting stained glass here, some medieval and some of later date.*) Back on main route, having

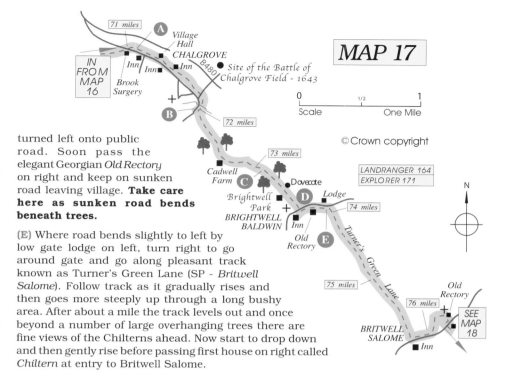

MAP 17

71 miles

Ⓐ Village Hall
CHALGROVE

IN FROM MAP 16

Inn Inn Inn B480

Brook Surgery

● Site of the Battle of Chalgrove Field - 1643

Ⓑ

72 miles

0   1/2   1
Scale   One Mile

© Crown copyright

73 miles

Cadwell Farm Ⓒ

● Dovecote

LANDRANGER 164
EXPLORER 171

N

Brightwell Park
BRIGHTWELL BALDWIN Inn

Lodge Ⓓ

74 miles

Old Rectory Ⓔ

Turner's Green Lane

75 miles

76 miles

Old Rectory

BRITWELL SALOME

SEE MAP 18

■ Inn

turned left onto public road. Soon pass the elegant Georgian *Old Rectory* on right and keep on sunken road leaving village. **Take care here as sunken road bends beneath trees.**

(E) Where road bends slightly to left by low gate lodge on left, turn right to go around gate and go along pleasant track known as Turner's Green Lane (SP - *Britwell Salome*). Follow track as it gradually rises and then goes more steeply up through a long bushy area. After about a mile the track levels out and once beyond a number of large overhanging trees there are fine views of the Chilterns ahead. Now start to drop down and then gently rise before passing first house on right called *Chiltern* at entry to Britwell Salome.

(F) At end of Turner's Green Lane, turn left with care (with pub called The Goose across road to right) to go down narrow verge on left-hand side of busy B4009, passing phone box on left. (There is a safer track running parallel to left of road, but this is not a right-of-way.) After about 100 yards turn left, off road, through small wooden gate up to left. Go down right-hand edge of field with hedge on immediate right. At bottom of field, by transformer on pole, go through small wooden gate and veer slightly left to go along road with pond to right. Pass

long, low barn on left and at end of barn, where church is visible ahead, bear right and immediately turn right to go through small wooden gate, with the Old Rectory over to left. *The Church of St Nicholas, with its little west bellcote, was entirely rebuilt in 1867.* Go along top, left-hand edge of field, making part-use of track, but then go straight ahead where track veers to right continuing along left-hand edge of field.

Turner's Green Lane descending towards Britwell Salome

(A) Over rudimentary stile beside metal gate and **cross the fast and busy B4009 with great care**. Turn right to go along left-hand verge of road, immediately passing Britwell Salome entry sign. Just beyond sign turn left (SP - *Bridleway*) to go up driveway with Cooper's Farm on left. Beyond farmyard keep in same direction on now roughly surfaced, gently rising track, bordered with possibly high hedges. *Good views of Chiltern slopes soon visible ahead.* Go through open space, veer slightly right and onto more overgrown path through bushes. Path soon gently rising all the way in woodland, first a narrow belt and then more extensive woodland to right.

Our 30-mile route between Britwell Salome and Burnham Beeches passes through the Chiltern Hills Area of Outstanding Natural Beauty, notable for its chalk hills, beech woodlands and flower-covered meadows. Red Kites, the spectacular birds of prey introduced in the 1990s are a familiar sight as they soar overhead.

To obtain further information visit: www.chilternsaonb.org

(B) About a mile beyond Cooper's Farm turn left onto track (SP - *Ridgeway Path*). *The Ridgeway Path is an 85-mile National Trail following the prehistoric ridge track between Overton Hill in Wiltshire and Ivinghoe Beacon in Buckinghamshire. From here it is possible to extend north-eastwards along the Icknield Way to Suffolk. Note signboard telling the story of Red Kites in the Chilterns. Keep an eye open for these magnificent birds - you should see several in the next few miles.* If track wet and muddy use footpath parallel to the track's right (SP - *Alternative Footpath - Walkers Only*). This runs through bushes just to the right of the track and appears to be kept clear. Keep along tree-lined track or path to a point where path re-joins track and continue along track. After half-a-mile pass entrance gates to large houses (Lys Farmhouse, but not signed) on right and after 40 paces --

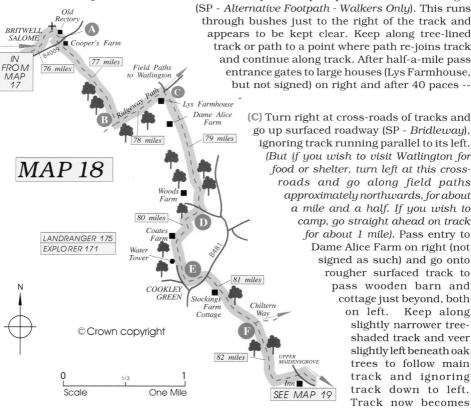

MAP 18

LANDRANGER 175
EXPLORER 171

© Crown copyright

N

0   1/2   1
Scale   One Mile

(C) Turn right at cross-roads of tracks and go up surfaced roadway (SP - *Bridleway*), ignoring track running parallel to its left. *(But if you wish to visit Watlington for food or shelter, turn left at this cross-roads and go along field paths approximately northwards, for about a mile and a half. If you wish to camp, go straight ahead on track for about 1 mile).* Pass entry to Dame Alice Farm on right (not signed as such) and go onto rougher surfaced track to pass wooden barn and cottage just beyond, both on left. Keep along slightly narrower tree-shaded track and veer slightly left beneath oak trees to follow main track and ignoring track down to left. Track now becomes

pleasant sunken pathway overhung with trees and gently rising all the way. Now into our first Chiltern beech wood - a foretaste of several more to come. Pass track coming up from the left and follow well-used path up slope, first veering to left. This wide, well-used path up through beech woods is waymarked by a series of white waymark arrows painted on trees. *These most helpful arrows are the work of the very vital Chiltern Society*

Woodland path beyond Dame Alice Farm

and originally pre-date the now conventional way-mark arrows found elsewhere. Occasional glimpses of Chiltern slopes down through trees to left. At end of wood, after our long climb up onto the Chilterns' top, turn left onto track by Woods Farm letterbox on right and pass horse paddocks on left.

(D) After 150 yards cross public road with care and veer slightly right to go down road (SP - *Private Road - Footpath only*). Pass woodland on right and follow road as it bends left and then right. Pass Coates Farm (not signed) farmhouse and barns to right and then bear gently left at crossing of tracks onto now rougher surfaced roadway, passing large wooden shed on left. Woods now on right and then on both sides. Pass large concrete water-tower in wood on right. Through modest gateway and pass semi-detached houses on left at entry to Cookley Green.

(E) On arrival at large village green turn left just before Jubilee seat on grass ahead. Walk along left-hand edge of green, but keeping just to right of row of pine trees bordering a private drive. Pass two cottages on left and **cross busy B481 with great care** before turning left to walk along its right-hand verge for about 35 paces. Now turn right down surfaced driveway (SP - *The Chiltern Way*). *The Chiltern Way is a 125-mile circular route with two extensions and takes in most of the Chilterns. It is organised by the Chiltern Society. We shall use a short section of it from here.* Pass large house on right and Stockings Farm Cottage just beyond, thus leaving Cookley Green. Driveway now becomes narrow bridleway. Ignore waymarked stile on left. Keep down pleasant bridleway overhung with trees, dropping down all the way, **but beware of exposed tree-roots** - the compiler stubbed his toe here!

Cookley Green

(F) At junction of paths, veer slightly right (SP - *SW 14*), keeping in almost the same direction as previously, and leaving the Chiltern Way which turns to go up left. Continue to drop gently down valley floor and after about 250 yards ignore unsigned footpath to right bordered with wooden gates and near power-pole. After about half-a-mile turn left at crossing of paths in slightly more open area to go over stile. Go up left-hand edge of very steep field - *the steepest we have encountered so far - but take heart, there are lovely valley views behind and a pub not far ahead!* Bear right to go along top of field and after about 50 paces turn left to go over stile. Up short slippery path in bushes and over stile to go up along fenced path on left-hand edge of field. Over stile and up path passing stable on right.

(A) Over stile and turn right **with care** onto public road at entry to Upper Maidensgrove hamlet. Pass the hospitable Five Horseshoes Inn on right and go along right-hand verge of public road leaving Upper Maidensgrove. Now go along left-hand verge of unfenced road with the extensive Maidensgrove and Russell's Water Commons to left. Pass entry drive to Nuthall Farm on left and entrance to Cookley Hill Farm on right. Pass noticeboard on left indicating Maidensgrove and Russell's Water Commons.

Our path along the edge of Stonor Park

(B) After about 130 paces, where road bends to left, go straight ahead along right-hand edge of common with trees and bracken to right. At end of common keep straight on track and soon bear right to go down road in Maidensgrove. Go straight, not left, by entrance to Island Cottage well over to left. Soon bear right onto minor public road by water hydrant. Pass entry to The White House on right. Bear left beyond Lodge Farm Cottage on left, with path down to right leading to the entry to the Warburg Nature Reserve. We have now re-joined the Oxfordshire Way (*see page 27*) for a very short distance.

(C) Immediately beyond entrance gates to Lodge Farm, turn left up track passing cottage on left and leaving Maidensgrove (SP - *PS 17*). *We have re-joined the Chiltern Way (see page 43).* Go into field and immediately bear right, *leaving the Oxfordshire Way*, to follow well-defined path across field towards woods. *Fine open views over to right, sometimes as far as the Surrey Hills.* Go over waymarked stile to follow well-defined path (waymarked with intermittent white arrows on trees) down through very attractive beech wood. Veer slightly right onto less defined path near end of wood and go over stile. Go down field aiming to left of lower spinney projecting from right. *Fine views of Stonor House in valley ahead left.* Over stile in cross-hedge and keep in same direction, straight down field on well-defined path, aiming just to right of power-pole. Over stile and down narrow tree-shaded path between wooden fence on right and yew trees on left.

Stonor House and Chapel

(D) Turn left **with care along the busy B480** at our entry to Stonor (SP - *Chiltern Way*). Probably use right-hand verge initially and almost immediately ignore bridleway to right, keeping up road. Before reaching bend to right probably go over to left-hand side of road - slightly safer! Ignore road to left and eventually pass house on left called Parkside. After 25 paces **cross road with great care** and go through tall kissing gate into Stonor Deer Park (Signed - *Keep dogs on lead*). *But walk*

44

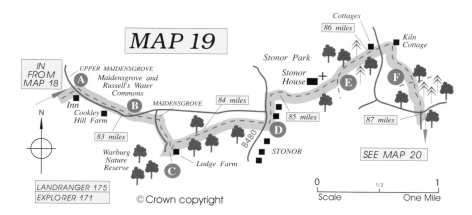

MAP 19

IN FROM MAP 18

UPPER MAIDENSGROVE
Maidensgrove and Russell's Water Commons

A

N

Inn
Cookley Hill Farm

B

MAIDENSGROVE

83 miles

84 miles

Warburg Nature Reserve

Lodge Farm

C

STONOR

B480

Stonor Park

Stonor House

85 miles

D

Cottages

86 miles

Kiln Cottage

E

F

87 miles

SEE MAP 20

LANDRANGER 175
EXPLORER 171

© Crown copyright

0   1/2   1
Scale   One Mile

further up the road if you wish to visit often open Stonor House - see below. Go straight up slope, aiming to immediate left of wire deer-fence coming in from right. From corner of deer-fence follow long path, first up and then along slope to immediate left of fence, with delightful views down to left, first of the park and then of impressive Stonor House. *Family home of the Stonors for over eight hundred years, this lovely mellow-brick mansion with a medieval chapel, in which this staunchly Roman Catholic family have always celebrated mass. The interior of the house is full of interest and there is a tearoom.* Pass gate in deer-fence to right. Just beyond top of fairly steep section of path enter woodland and go through tall kissing gate in deer-fence. Keep in same direction through different type of woodland with some rhododendrons, conifers and silver birch.

(E) Veer slightly to right beyond tree with CW painted in white, joining track coming in from left. Now keep on track as it gently climbs up wooded valley. At junction of tracks veer right along track, which goes well to right of possible

Having now entered Buckingham-shire we shall now come across these elegant symbols almost as far as the outskirts of London.

white way-mark arrow on tree. At this point we leave Oxfordshire and enter Buckinghamshire (*see inset*). Keep along track passing semi-detached cottages on left, the first one being No 42. Go straight across public road **with care** onto surfaced driveway (SP - *Public Footpath*). Follow track as it bends to right passing metal gate to Kiln Cottage on left and where it bends to left, go straight ahead to go over stile beside large wooden gate. *Please note sign asking for your respect for the environment.* (The next three route directions may look a little complicated, but take them one at a time and all will be clear!) Go along right-hand edge of field and after 40 paces turn right to go over stile and then immediately left to go down left-hand edge of field. After about 60 paces beyond end of spinney projecting from left and just beyond power-line, turn left to go over stile and then turn right to go along right-hand edge of field with hedge now on immediate right.

(F) Towards end of field start to drop down and then go over stile to go steeply down, inside the right-hand edge of woods. Cross over bridleway track in bottom of valley and go up opposite path through largely coniferous Gussetts Wood. Follow path as it eventually veers up to the right following white waymark arrow on tree. Over stile at end of wood and go straight across field soon identifying stile as it comes into view to left of large wooden gate.

45

(A) Over this stile and go straight over road junction to go down minor public road (SP - *Fawley*) with pleasant woodland to left. After about 400 yards pass wooden barns on left and just beyond, fork left off road by asbestos barns of Upper Woodend Farm on left and go down concrete farm road (SP - *Bridleway*). Pass house on right, follow farm road as it veers to left and at its end, bear right on to bridleway with overhanging bushes. Now starting to drop very gently down. Pass stile on left which carries a path crossing our bridleway. At end of bushes veer slightly right to follow path into woods and after about 60 paces veer right, to go on path around probably boggy sunken section. Turn left on edge of wood by metal gate on right and down steep and possibly slippery slope before bearing right to re-join sunken bridleway. At end of sunken section veer slightly right and follow path down through magnificent beech woods.

Track down to Hambleden

(B) At crossing of tracks in valley bottom go almost straight across to follow track up steep slope, soon curving to right. Keep on track, ignoring small footpath signed to left. Pleasant glimpses of richly wooded valley down to right. Pass waymark sign on left and at about 60 paces beyond it, fork right to go under yew tree (*White waymark arrow on tree*) onto grassier track. Fork left at next Y-junction of tracks onto grassier of the two, which bends round to left. Turn right at T-junction of tracks (*White waymark arrow on tree*) with metal gate visible well over to left. Now on level and better surfaced track, still in magnificent beech wood.

(C) Turn left at crossing of tracks, go out of wood on track and keep in same direction across field aiming for left-hand edge of wood ahead. *Fine views of the Hamble Valley ahead.* On reaching wood on right keep down track to its immediate left for about 30 paces before turning right through gap into wood and go down path within the left-hand edge of wood. Now starting to drop down quite steeply. At bottom of wood go over cross-roads of tracks and keep down track. Just beyond garage of The Bell House on right, turn right onto busy minor road and **cross to its left-hand verge with great care**. Keep along road passing Hambleden entry sign.

(D) Pass gates to

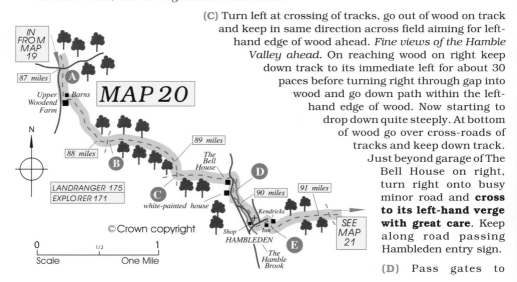

IN FROM MAP 19

87 miles

A

Upper Woodend Farm

Barns

MAP 20

N

88 miles

B

89 miles

The Bell House

D

LANDRANGER 175
EXPLORER 171

C

white-painted house

90 miles

91 miles

©Crown copyright

Kendricks

SEE MAP 21

Shop

HAMBLEDEN

Inn

E

The Hamble Brook

0   1/2   1
Scale   One Mile

unsigned white house on right and after about 75 paces turn left to go over stile. Then bear right to go across field aiming for stile just to right of small, mellow-brick bridge. Over this stile and turn left to go on minor public road to cross bridge over the little Hamble Brook. Just beyond bridge ignore kissing gate on left and keep on road, thus re-joining the Chiltern Way.

Now entering the very attractive village of Hambleden. Leave road by bearing slightly left, through small wooden gate into churchyard and keep in same direction along pathway just to right of church tower. *Note the elaborate mid-18th-century Kenrick Mausoleum over to left.* Bear left beyond the handsome tower and go down churchyard path. *But turn left if you wish to visit church. This has a rather stark interior, the result of restoration in the 19th century, but it contains several items of interest including a cylindrical Norman font and an interesting monument in the north transept, in memory of Sir Cope D'Oyley. Husband and wife face each other,*

Hambleden Church

while their many children kneel below. The two eldest boys are dressed as Royalists, while the others are depicted as Parliamentarians - evidence of the many families divided by the tragedy of the Civil War. The skulls in the hands of several of the children indicate that they pre-deceased their parents. Leave churchyard through lychgate and turn left to pass War Memorial (but bear right if you wish to visit very useful shop). At end of churchyard wall, go straight, not left, up road passing private house still signed *Wheeler's Butchery*, and the Stag and Huntsman Inn, both on right. Pass turning to car park on right and keep up hill on private road (access allowed to walkers as this is a right-of-way).

(E) After about 150 paces, just before reaching Kenricks (house) ahead on right, turn right onto track. Turn left just beyond private wooden steps up to left, onto path between hedge on left and fence on right (SP - *Chiltern Way*). Climb up path quite steeply with fine views back across the Hamble Valley, with woods soon on left and then on both sides. Just before end of wood go over track (*Footpath waymark*) and follow slender white posts to reach stile on edge of wood. Go over this stile and keep along left-hand edge of field with wood still to immediate left for about 70 yards. Where wood ends on left bear slightly right to go along grassy track, aiming just to left of oak tree and power pole. Now in reasonably flat, upland country (but not for very long!). Go through two sets of metal gates crossing surfaced track (SP - *Chiltern Way*) (use stiles if gates closed) and keep along grassy track. Farm buildings and houses of Rotten Row hamlet visible ahead left.

The D'Oyley Monument, Hambleden Church

(A) At end of track bear left to go up narrow public road **with great care** (SP - *Chiltern Way*). Soon enter Rotten Row hamlet ignoring footpath signed to right just before first house on right. Pass pretty pond on right and neat farmhouse and buildings on left. Just beyond pond go straight ahead leaving public road, which bends to left. Go along short concrete roadway (SP - *Chiltern Way*) and go over stile beside metal gate. Veer very slightly left to go across field aiming for stile

Pond at Rotten Row

in cross-fence when it becomes visible. Over double stile and keep in same direction across next field eventually aiming for stile and metal gate at edge of wood, not visible until after some yards. Over this stile into wood and go down track for 35 paces before going over a second stile and turning right onto minor public road (still in woodland) (SP - *Chiltern Way*). Keep on road ignoring footpath signed to left thereby temporarily leaving the Chiltern Way.

(B) Turn left, off road, to go onto shared drive of Woodside House and Homefield Hall for about 10 paces and then turn left again to go into wood. Now follow path around to right and right again going well behind the garden of Homefield Hall. Go along ill-defined path dropping down slope and passing white waymark arrow on tree. Soon bear left to go more steeply down, passing another white waymark arrow on tree. Veer a little more to left to go over small stile in cross-fence and keep in same direction beyond it. Turn right in valley bottom onto broad, grassy track, re-joining the Chiltern Way (but not signed here). Now in

Homefield Wood, eventually passing Nature Reserve noticeboard on left, just beyond track up to left. Nature Reserve with broadleaf trees now on left until passing a second noticeboard on left just before going through gap and over small parking area.

(C) Turn right immediately beyond parking area onto minor public road (SP - *Chiltern Way*) and follow it up to right **with great care** for about 60 paces. Now turn left, off bend in road, to go over stile beside metal gate (SP - *Chiltern Way*). Go down right-hand edge of field in this now more open valley and over stile beside metal gate to go up right-hand edge of next field. Well before reaching metal gate turn right to go over stile (SP - *Chiltern Way*) and keep on long, narrow pathway along side of valley, with fence and field to right and hedge to left. At end of long, narrow path, go over stile (SP - *Chiltern Way*) into Davenport Wood (*partly owned by the Woodland Trust, as notice indicates*). After a few paces go straight over crossing of paths and up steep path in woods beyond. (*NB - These woods require careful navigation as there is at present a mixture of waymarks, not all of which point in our direction. If in doubt follow the white arrow waymarks*

Our path through Davenport Wood

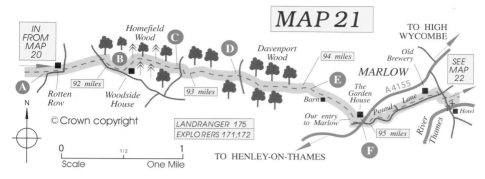

MAP 21

IN FROM MAP 20

Homefield Wood **C**

B

D

Davenport Wood

94 miles

TO HIGH WYCOMBE

Old Brewery

SEE MAP 22

MARLOW

E

A4155

A

92 miles

Rotten Row

Woodside House

93 miles

Barn

The Garden House

Pound Lane

Hotel

© Crown copyright

Our entry to Marlow

95 miles

River Thames

N

LANDRANGER 175
EXPLORERS 171,172

F

0   1/2   1
Scale   One Mile

TO HENLEY-ON-THAMES

on trees - they are usually a reliable indicator of our path's direction.). Pass tree with white waymark arrows and veer to left at junction of paths following another white waymark arrow on tree.

(D) Go straight over minor public road by small car parking area (SP - *Chiltern Way*) and veer slightly to right following white arrow waymark on tree, then right again by small waymark post. Pass faded white waymark arrow on tree and veer left searching ahead with care for the next one. Go over boundary ditch and veer to right beyond it following white waymark on tree. Course of our path now becomes much clearer. Go straight over crossing of paths and start to drop down a little - this gradual descent will be maintained almost all the way to Marlow, less than two miles ahead. Bear right at inverted Y-junction of paths onto track. After about 70 paces ignore path to right. Soon cross another pathway, first veering left and then bearing right, to go straight down fenced track beyond woods, ignoring two stiles to right. Wood still up to left of track and field down to its right.

(E) Bear right at junction of paths to go down fenced path with outskirts of Marlow visible well ahead. After about 250 yards ignore path to right starting at metal ladder-stile. Now go under trees passing wooden barn on right and at end of trees ignore path up to left. Pass houses on right at our entry to Marlow and go through metal kissing gate onto short track. Bear left with care onto minor public road with houses now on both sides. Pass The Garden House on left.

(F) Go straight across the busy A4155 with great care and down Pound Lane. Now keep along the built-up, meandering, but clearly defined Pound Lane ignoring various fish-titled closes to left and right - *Trout, Perch, Pike, Bream, etc..* Pass sports ground on right. Go straight over two mini-roundabouts, the second with large car park to its right. Pass old brewery up to left - now luxury flats. Pass park with children's play area and toilets on right. At end of Pound Lane, turn right at mini-roundabout onto busier road and **cross this with great care** to arrive at War Memorial. (*But turn left here if you wish to explore the bustling market town of Marlow, with bright shops, restaurants, inns and hotels at its largely Georgian centre.*) Now move to Chapter 4.

Our path down to Marlow

Chapter 4 Marlow to West Drayton

(A) Continue south-eastwards from Marlow's War Memorial towards the church, immediately passing the George and Dragon on left. Pass the Rectory on left with lovely old sundial above its entry doorway. *But go straight ahead if you wish to visit the Parish Church, bridge and riverside. The tall-spired church is almost entirely Victorian, but is worth visiting for its monuments, the best of which is that to Sir Miles Hobart. This is complete with a relief sculpture depicting the coach accident which led to his death. The Thames flows by immediately beyond the church and is crossed here by an elegant suspension bridge (1831-6) - the work of William Tierney Clarke, who also designed a similar bridge linking Buda and Pest.* On main route - go only a single pace into churchyard before turning left along its left-hand edge, re-joining the Thames Path (*see page 32*), which we shall now follow as far as Cookham (SP - *Thames Path*). Go along passage with red-brick wall to right and, at its end, veer right to cross road with care and almost immediately turn left just beyond the Two Brewers Inn. (*You may wish to go down this road a few yards to look across the Thames to the Compleat Angler Hotel and Marlow's suspension bridge, to its right.*) Go down narrow, twisting and turning pathway between high brick walls and at its end turn right with care to go down public road. Ignore turning to Thamesfield Gardens on left. Pass path to usually busy Marlow Lock on right (*you might wish to go down here for a few minutes*). Keep straight on, down Mill Road, passing Marlow Mill (now flats) on right and bending to left.

(B) At 30 paces beyond bend to left after Marlow Mill, turn right onto path (SP - *Thames Path*) and soon veer left to go on path across park and veer left again to go parallel with Thames, now down to right. At end of park continue along towpath with river to right and a few houses to left. Now leave Marlow and go across meadow and under large concrete bridge beneath the noisy A404. Keep on path with fence now to left and Thames to right. *Good easy walking here after all the ups and downs across the Chilterns!* Steep wooded slopes of Winter Hill over to right, beyond the Thames, as we bend to left following the towpath. Pass two exotic houses on far bank of Thames, the second with elaborate castellations, but not of any great age. Pass fine avenue of poplar trees on left, in a parkland setting with mown grass and several seats and picnic tables. Keep along towpath, much of which is shaded by willows. Go through five metal kissing gates in succession, across broad meadows, following the Thames, which gradually veers away from the now barer slopes of Winter Hill. A few houses are on the far shore of the Thames, but our bank is completely clear. Note railway line running parallel over to our left. Now go along towpath across larger meadow and at its end

MAP 22

LANDRANGER 175
EXPLORER 172

IN FROM MAP 21

MARLOW

TO HIGH WYCOMBE AND M40

Rly. Stn.

TO MAIDENHEAD AND M4

Winter Hill

96 miles

97 miles

98 miles

River Thames

'A few houses'

99 miles

Spade Oak Meadow

TO MARLOW

Inn

Sailing Club

Marina

A4094

TO BEACONSFIELD

BOURNE END

Rly. Stn.

Cock Marsh Meadow

100 miles

Sailing Club

COOKHAM

SEE MAP 23

TO MAIDENHEAD

©Crown copyright

N

0   1/2   1
Scale   One Mile

50

Marlow's Riverside

go through metal kissing gate into Spade Oak Meadow, the last one before reaching Bourne End.

(C) Through metal kissing gate at end of Spade Oak Meadow and go across surfaced area with railway level-crossing gates over to left. (Spade Oak Inn just beyond level-crossing.) Now continue along surfaced towpath at our effective entry to Bourne End (SP - *Thames Path*) passing chalets to left and gardens to right. *Bourne End is popular with dinghy sailors and the river here will often be colourfully alive with their activity.* Through gate to cross lawn in front of Upper Thames Sailing Club, noting (*but only in summer*) handsome bust of King Neptune over to left. *Good views to right over the Thames to meadowland and hill slopes beyond.* Through gate at end of club to go down shady towpath beyond, before emerging into the Bourne End Marina with moorings to right and modern housing to left. Over small bridge crossing branch of marina and pass cafe on left. Bear right just beyond and leave marina to go down narrow pathway.

(D) Turn right on meeting blue-brick bridge (SP - *Thames Path*), go up steps and cross Thames by footway attached to railway bridge alongside on left. Down steps, turn right and right again to go along towpath, with Thames now to left. After a few paces go through wooden kissing gate into the National Trust's Cockmarsh Meadow, noting interesting information board over to right. Keep along towpath partly shaded by willow trees. We have now left Bourne End although there are still some substantial houses on the opposite bank of the Thames. Go through metal kissing gate at end of Cockmarsh Meadow and, well beyond it, go beneath lovely old tree as Thames and towpath start to bend gently round to left and Cookham Bridge comes into view well ahead. Go onto concrete pathway in front of sailing club and house beyond and then onto tree-shaded pathway with grassy area to right and the Thames to left, ignoring path signed to right. This is our entry to the village of Cookham.

The Thames from Spade Oak Meadow, near Point C

51

(A) At end of grassy area, by weeping willow trees at our entry to Cookham, go straight ahead, keeping on towpath (*But turn right if you wish to visit Cookham Church, the entrance to its churchyard being only 70 paces away. The church has a stout 16th-century tower and an impressively spacious, but much restored interior. See especially the poignant monument to Sir Isaac Pocock, by the noted sculptor, John Flaxman, showing Sir Isaac in the arms of an angel on a boat; he died while boating on the Thames. Cookham will always be best known for its connections with the controversial artist, Stanley Spencer and there is a copy of his painting,* The Last Supper *hanging in the church. Walk into the village if you wish to visit the interesting Stanley Spencer Gallery.*) Turn right in front of Ferry Cottage (SP - *Cookham Village*), go along short, narrow pathway and turn left up steps just beyond. Turn left **with great care** to go along pathway on left-hand side of the busy A4094 (*but go across this road **with great care** if you wish to visit the Ferry Inn*). Cross narrow Cookham Bridge over the Thames on left-hand pathway.

(B) After 150 paces turn right to cross road **with great care** to go over stile at the start of the Beeches Way (SP - *The Beeches Way* - in future referred to as *BW*). **To avoid waymark duplication we shall rely, in certain areas, solely on Beeches Way waymarks.** We shall now follow the Beeches Way for almost all of its course until reaching the Grand Union Canal at West Drayton. This path was the idea of Lorna Atkinson and was developed by the Iver and District

Hedsor Church

Countryside Association. Having gone over stile at the start of the Beeches Way, head diagonally across field aiming just to right of Lord Boston's Folly (see below) on a hill beyond. Soon go alongside field edge on right with a branch of the Thames immediately beyond trees on right. *This area is still known as Hedsor Wharf, but it must be many years since any barges have docked here.* Now follow right-hand edge of field with Thames eventually bending away to right. Now follow wooden fence on right and at end of field veer slightly right to go over wooden bridge crossing stream. Veer right to go along private road passing ambitious house and buildings on right. Veer left at junction of private roads and go up path on left-hand side of road. Go through small wooden gate to left of large wooden gates, passing unusual thatched house on left.

(C) Go straight over busy public road **with great care** to go through gates onto private drive with Victorian lodge on left (SP - *Hedsor Priory* and *BW*). Good view of 18th-century Lord Boston's Folly, on hill ahead left, with its three flint towers and curtain walling. *Pass small*

Littleworth Common

gate on right, with steep path up across field beyond, to the attractive little church of St Nicholas with its pyramid-roofed bell-turret. Usually locked but its churchyard is a wonderfully tranquil place to stop awhile and there are fine views across to the folly and over the Thames Valley, back towards Marlow. Continue up drive and just before white-painted gate veer left off drive through metal kissing gate (SP - *BW*). Go up path with fences on both sides, climbing up away from the

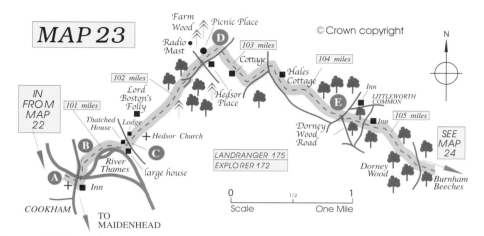

MAP 23

Farm Wood
Picnic Place
Radio Mast
D
103 miles
Cottage
104 miles
Hales Cottage
Inn
LITTLEWORTH COMMON
102 miles
Lord Boston's Folly
Hedsor Place
E
IN FROM MAP 22
101 miles
Thatched House
Lodge
Hedsor Church
Dorney Wood Road
Inn
105 miles
B
C
River Thames
large house
Dorney Wood
SEE MAP 24
A
Inn
Burnham Beeches
COOKHAM
TO MAIDENHEAD

LANDRANGER 175
EXPLORER 172

0   1/2   1
Scale   One Mile

Thames Valley and into woodlands. Keep straight ahead on track where another track comes in from right After about 100 paces go through gateway and veer right onto better surfaced track. After about another 100 paces pass house on right and at end of private roadway go straight ahead **with great care** to go beside public road (No Sign). Pass houses on left and soon go over cross-roads, keeping on public road. Pass Hedsor Place on right and radio mast well over to left. Pass entry to Farm Wood on left, with useful picnic tables.

(D) After about 100 paces beyond Farm Wood turn right onto path (SP - *BW*) and go along, inside, right-hand edge of wood. Pass attractive brick-built cottage on right and keep in same direction on track beyond. Hedge now on right and line of trees on left. At end of track turn left onto public road and keep along road with woods on both sides. Turn right at road T-junction (SP - *Burnham Beeches*) and pass entrance to Hales Cottage on left with lions on its gateway. At the end of a long beech hedge and where road bends to left, turn left, off road to go along pathway through spinney. Over stile and veer slightly left to go across field on hopefully well-defined path. At end of field go over stile and veer slightly right to go along right-hand edge of woodlands, with fields to right.

(E) At end of path go through kissing gate and go left to cross public road **with care**. Almost immediately turn right into Dorney Wood Road. After 40 paces turn left onto path into wood (SP - *B W*). Soon emerge from wood to follow well-defined path across open bracken-covered space of Littleworth Common and then back into wood for a few yards. Emerge from wood to veer right across small car park with very welcome Blackwood Arms pub over to left. Cross minor public road beyond car park and over stile beside metal gate (SP - *BW*). Go along short grassy track and over second stile beside second metal gate. Go along right-hand side of field with wood on right and over stile. Go down fenced path with fields to left and right and through kissing gate onto clearly defined path up through Dorney Wood (notice indicates *The Portman Burtley Estate*). Bear slightly right onto wider track before going over stile. Cross minor public road with care and over small car park just beyond, near entry to Burnham Beeches (*not signed here*).

The Blackwood Arms, Littleworth Common

(A) Now entering the Burnham Beeches Estate, but not signed here *(no waymarks within this estate)*. The historic landscape of Burnham Beeches covers an area of over 500 acres and prior to the Dissolution of the Monasteries in 1539, belonged to Burnham Abbey. In 1879 the whole area was purchased by the Corporation of London and this body continues to manage it. Much of these

High Summer in Burnham Beeches

magnificent beech wood-lands are pollarded and this not only produces a continuous crop of wood but also increases the life of the trees. After a short distance our path will follow the surfaced Halse Drive, but there are many quieter paths leading off it for those who have the time and energy to spare. Pass dog-loo box on right and keep straight on along path with rhododendron bushes on both sides. Over cross-roads at large Hartley Court Moat signboard describing Burnham Beeches Estate and pass small log shelter on right. Join surfaced roadway soon passing sign indicating that we are on Halse Drive. This tarmac roadway may seem rather bland but it runs through magnificent beech woods. Past turning to Woods Drive on right, Duke's Drive on left. Pass two useful benches on right as we drop downhill.

(B) Over cross-roads in valley, with Victoria Drive to right and Burnham Walk (not indicated here) to left, the latter with a small wooden shelter beside it a few yards away. Go fairly steeply up far side of valley, still on Halse Drive. At end of Halse Drive bear right to go through gap beside large wooden gate; now in car-user area. Fork left beyond small car park area and bear left again at next road junction by car park and refreshment hut beyond, both on right. *Refreshment hut open seasonally and more often at weekends; this can provide a useful free leaflet as well as refreshments.* Keep straight along surfaced roadway of Lord Mayor's Drive, although it is possible to walk parallel with it to right. Pass large car park on right - rejoin road here if you have used grass to right. Pass large noticeboard on right indicating entry to the Corporation of London's Burnham Beeches National Nature Reserve, which we are now just leaving. Over cross-roads just beyond noticeboard (SP - *Farnham Common*) and go along right-hand pavement beside Beeches Road at entry to Farnham Common village.

(C) Turn right at T-junction in centre of bustling Farnham Common village to go alongside very busy A355 (SP - *Slough*) and soon turn left to cross to left-hand side of road at controlled crossing. Keep in same direction passing useful shops and restaurants. Pass Stag and Hounds Inn on left and immediately beyond the Foresters Inn on left, turn left off A355, into Victoria Road. Pass Victoria Inn on left and turn right just beyond Village Hall on right to go along Parsonage Lane. After 60 paces turn left to go through gap onto narrow path (SP - *BW*), first with hedges on both sides and then with wooden garden fences on both sides.

(D) Keep along path, bearing slightly right into Brockhurst Woods (not indicated here) and still keep within fences, mostly on both sides. (*Brockhurst Woodlands are private, please keep to path or track all the way to their end, where we shall go over stile into field, some way ahead.*) Keep on path as it drops gently downwards to valley, where we cross small bridge over minute stream. Veer slightly left beyond bridge to go up steep bank keeping just to right of wire fence and watching out for exposed tree-roots! With wire fence still to left, soon go parallel with wire-mesh fence also on right, with garden beyond it. Over stile beside wooden gate and pass entrance to Hornbeam Cottage on right, keeping in same direction along the cottage's approach drive. Go between brick pillars (SP - *BW*) and soon veer left across drive which leads to second cottage back left and then turn left onto track on right-hand edge of wood, with trees also on its right-hand side. After about 200 yards turn right to follow edge of wood and after 100 yards turn left to follow edge of wood.

(E) After about 250 yards turn right to go over stile (SP - *BW*) finally leaving Brockhurst Woods and go down right-hand edge of field with fence on immediate right. Over stile beside wooden gate and **with care, cross minor public road** (*Duffield Lane, but not indicated here*). Through metal kissing gate opposite (SP - *BW*) and go up path, initially overhung by fine oak trees, but rather spoilt by corrugated iron fence on right. Through wooden kissing gate and keep in

In Brockhurst Wood beyond Farnham Common

same direction, going over cross-path. Keep in same direction along path through low woodlands, going almost due east. Veer slightly right in open area where gate is visible well over to left. Almost immediately turn right (SP - *BW*) into woodlands again. Go through wooden kissing gate and turn left onto grassy track.

(F) Through wooden kissing gate and **with great care go straight over busy road** (*Gerrards Cross Road, but not indicated here*). Go through small wooden gate and veer left to go to immediate right of Stoke Common information board. Go along wide path through low woodlands and keep on it as it emerges from woodlands into the more open Stoke Common. At junction of tracks turn right (SP - *BW*) to go along about half-a-mile of straight track across Stoke Common. Over crossing of tracks.

(G) At end of long stretch go over diagonal cross-roads of tracks (SP - *B W*) and now along the right-hand edge of a broad ride with woods beyond on both sides. Where gateway is visible well ahead, left, bear right onto finely surfaced horse-friendly track which meanders through woodlands. At junction of tracks turn left onto grassy path, less used by horses (*No Sign*). Follow path as it bends round to left (SP - *BW*) and go through small wooden gate before turning right **with great care** to go along right-hand side of busy road (SP - *BW*).

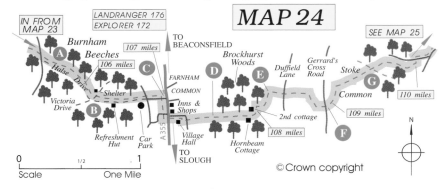

MAP 24

IN FROM MAP 23

LANDRANGER 176
EXPLORER 172

SEE MAP 25

Burnham Beeches

107 miles

TO BEACONSFIELD

Brockhurst Woods

Gerrard's Cross Road

Duffield Lane

Stoke

106 miles

C

FARNHAM COMMON

D

E

Halse Drive

Shelter

Victoria Drive

B

Inns & Shops

Common

G

110 miles

2nd cottage

109 miles

A355

Refreshment Hut

Car Park

Village Hall

Hornbeam Cottage

108 miles

F

N

TO SLOUGH

0   1/2   1
Scale   One Mile

© Crown copyright

Site of old conservatory in Langley Park

(A) Start to go down beside busy road and soon turn left onto even busier road (SP - *Gerrards Cross*) at our entry to the surprisingly unspoilt village of Fulmer, passing entrance gates to Fulmer Hall on left. **With great care**, cross to pavement on right-hand side as we drop down into Fulmer with its brick-built church tower soon visible ahead. Pass the colourful Black Horse Inn and the church, both on right. *The beautifully cared-for church was rebuilt by Sir Marmaduke Dayrell in the early years of the 17th century and he and his wife are remembered in an elaborate monument standing in the chancel, with their two recumbent figures above the kneeling figures of their children.* Just beyond church and phone box, turn right through kissing-gate beside large metal gate and along short driveway onto path. Go along path on left-hand edge of field with hedge on left and wooden fence on right.

(B) Through metal kissing gate beyond small plantation and veer left to go diagonally across field (SP - *BW*) aiming just to right of transformer on power-pole. At end of field go over stile to left of metal gate and beneath oak tree (SP - *BW*). Veer right to go diagonally right, across field, to go through metal kissing gate and over very small concrete bridge. Now go up field veering away from its right-hand edge (SP - *BW*) and through metal kissing gate onto narrow, often boggy path overhung by rhododendron bushes. At end of path go straight across private estate road onto another rhododendron-bordered path. Soon bear right onto winding private estate road. Pass a number of entrances to luxurious houses - Woodland Court on left, Upton House on right, Fulmer Common House on right, Fulmer Common Cottage on right and Downings on left. Through small gate beside large metal gates leaving Fulmer Rise Estate.

(C) Turn left with care **to walk with care along public road**. After 120 paces turn right at road junction and go along straight, tree-lined Black Park Road. After 300 paces, pass large metal gates on left and after a further 200 paces turn left, off road, and go over stile beside wooden gate into woodlands of Black Park Country Park (*not indicated here*) (SP - *BW*). Go along unsurfaced path and after about 300 paces turn right onto well-surfaced track. After about 150 paces cross small bridge over dry ditch with railings and after about a further 150 yards, meet wooden railings ahead. Here, with far end of field visible over to right, turn left to go down grassier track (SP - *BW*). Pass welcome bench on left and at 5-way junction of tracks by Black Park information board over to left, turn right onto better surfaced track and immediately fork left (SP - *BW*). (*The famous Pinewood Film Studios are less than a mile away from here - to the north-east. Naturalists will also be interested to learn that the Park has a rich insect life including 18 species of butterfly and a nationally rare cricket.*) Soon go over very small bridge with wooden rails and keep on track at next cross-roads of tracks. Pass open area to left, go over next crossing of tracks and veer right

Giant Redwoods in Langley Park

down path with wooden fence and woodlands to left.

(D) Arrive at shore of lake and follow path anti-clockwise around shore of very attractive lake formed by an unobtrusive dam at its south-western end, which our path follows. *This lake was once the source of water-power to a saw mill at Rowley Farm, some distance below the dam.* Over bridge crossing small outfall from lake. Veer right just past Visitor Centre (with refreshment facilities) away from lake. Through gap in wooden fence and go straight ahead along wide path through woodlands. Veer slightly left at crossing of tracks by an unusual wooden sculpture by Richard Jones entitled *Folly*.

(E) At the end of this very long path, turn right to go through gap in fence and **cross the very fast and busy**

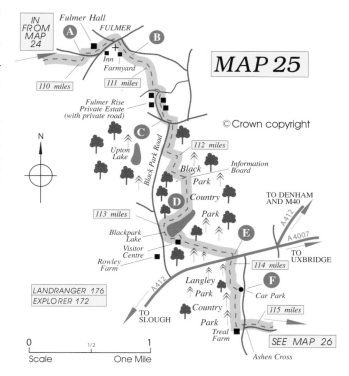

double-track A412 road with very great care. Go through metal gate (SP - *BW*) and onto path through woodlands entering Langley Park Country Park. (*The following series of route directions may appear complex, but follow each one carefully and you will eventually emerge into the vicinity of the Langley Park car park at* **F**.) Soon fork left through gap beside gateway (SP - *BW*). Keep straight ahead, ignoring path coming in from left. Go straight across junction of paths by tree in middle and soon fork right (SP- *Toilets*). Veer slightly left by start of brick-built ha-ha on left. Bear round to left to follow left-curving haha just to left. Through large wooden kissing gate into open area and keep veering round to left, soon passing disused wooden toilet building on right. Still keep veering left, parallel with ha-ha to left. Where surfaced track veers to right, pass open terrace over to left, where a large conservatory once stood. Keep bending round to left, leaving better-surfaced track. Ha-ha ends and soon go through large wooden gate back into woodlands. Immediately beyond gate, turn right down rhododendron-lined track. Turn left at T-junction of tracks and head along avenue of trees.

(F) Turn right, just before meeting Langley Park Country Park car park and go down wide grassy avenue with car park now to left (SP - *B W*). Continue southwards down this avenue of giant redwoods. Pass turn to Bennett's Walk on right. Through gap beside wooden gate and turn left by small Langley Park information board (SP - *BW* and *Billet Lane*). Keep along concrete path on left of roadway with wall to right passing immaculate Treal Farm on right. Go over public road at road junction at Ashen Cross (not signed) and go along public road opposite (SP - *BW*). Keep along this quiet minor road, soon becoming pleasantly overhung by trees.

(A) At T-junction at end of Bellswood Lane **cross busy road with great care, using traffic island down to right** and veering slightly right to go through metal kissing gate (SP - *BW*). Go along path overhung with bushes, with hedge on left being eventually replaced by fields on left and then fields on both sides. Veer slightly left to go onto surfaced roadway passing bungalow and salvage yard on right. Turn right to go beside public road at entry to Love Green (*not signed*) and after 80 paces turn left to

The Swan Inn, Iver

cross road **with great care** and go across left-hand edge of green with useful bench. Turn left onto public road by Love Green Garage and after about 50 paces turn right onto narrow pathway immediately beyond house on right (*temporarily leaving the course of the Beeches Way*) (SP - *Public Footpath*). Go across field with fences on both sides of path and at end of field veer slightly right to follow narrow path into Iver with garden fencing on both sides. *Would Iver like to be regarded as a town or a village? It has certainly grown apace in the last half of the 20th century, but there are a number of pleasant old houses in the area around the church and it still has a village flavour.*

(B) At end of path, turn left to go along left-hand pavement beside Iver High Street (B470). *Our walk through Iver of just under a mile is likely to be rather noisy but it allows access to many useful shops and is the most direct route for us to follow.* Pass school on left and cross to right-hand side **with great care** when the opportunity arises. Veer slightly right by mini-roundabout (SP - *Uxbridge*). Pass Chequers Inn on left and various useful shops on both sides.

(C) Turn right, off the High Street into Thorney Lane North (SP - *Ridgeway Trading Estate*) at small roundabout by Swan Inn on left and immediately afterwards, Iver Parish Church is then on left. *This has a heavily restored but spacious interior, the contents of which include an interesting Norman font, a large 17th-century monument in the chancel to Mary Salter, with her shrouded figure rising from her coffin and her children below. There is also a sad wall monument to a midshipman who died in Kingston, Jamaica aged only 15.* Having now re-joined the Beeches Way at the cross-roads we follow Thorney Lane North for about 300 yards before turning left into Victoria Crescent (SP - *BW*). Ignore loop road to left, passing green on left and at end of road veer right onto path and immediately left, passing house on

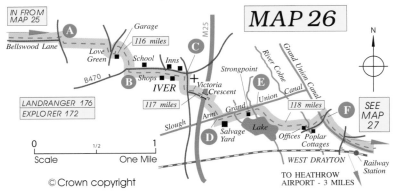

MAP 26

© Crown copyright

58

left with the figures of horses enlivening its gateway. Go down narrow fenced path and go up and across footbridge crossing the unbelievably noisy M25 motorway. Beyond footbridge bear right to go on concrete road with large sewage works on left.

(D) Over bridge crossing the Slough Arm of the Grand Union Canal. *This was completed in 1882 and, until recently, was the last stretch of new canal to be built in this country. It was built to link London with the great brickfields east of Slough.* Immediately beyond canal bridge, turn

Bridge over the M25 - not a pretty sight!

left to go down slope passing large salvage yard on right. At bottom of slope turn left to go through gap beside metal gate and turn right to follow towpath beside the canal. Over small aqueduct crossing Colnebrook, under high-voltage power-lines and go between metal barriers passing World War II strong-point. *Many of these strong-points were hastily erected in 1940 when invasion seemed imminent and most were built along the course of canals and rivers to provide crude defensive lines. Luckily they were never put to the test.* Over second small aqueduct crossing River Colne.

(E) On meeting footbridge No 1, fork right just before it to go up slope by stone pillar on right. *This is one of many coal duty posts which once indicated the boundary at which coal brought into the capital became liable to tax.* At top of slope bear right to go along gravel path with bushes on both sides (SP - *BW & Trout Lane*). Lake visible through trees to right - the result of old gravel workings. At path junction veer slightly left to go over bridge crossing waterway and beyond, bear left onto surfaced track. Bear right at inverted Y-junction onto surfaced road (SP - *West Drayton Station*). Pass Boyer Group offices on right and turn left by Poplar Cottages. Over bridge crossing Frays River and go straight, not right, ignoring turning to Tavistock Road. Keep on pavement on right-hand side of road and go over narrow hump-backed bridge **with great care** crossing Grand Union Canal. (*This waterway, originally known as the Grand Junction Canal, was built in the 18th century to provide a link between the Thames at Brentford and Braunston on the Oxford Canal. In 1927 it was amalgamated with a number of other canals and took the name Grand Union. We shall now be on its towpath for almost eleven miles. From here onwards there are no Shakespeare's Way waymarks - the canal towpath route is easy to follow and beyond it, unless otherwise instructed, follow Thames Path waymarks.*)

(F) Immediately beyond bridge turn very sharp right to go down steps and turn left to go along towpath with canal now on immediate right.Pass Union Wharf flats and offices on right (*not named*) and go under bridge. *But if you wish to miss out the walk into London (which would be a pity), turn left to go up slope, go over bridge, along road into West Drayton and turn left at road junction to arrive at West Drayton Station. From here there are frequent services to Paddington Station in central London. From Paddington it is possible to take a tube train to Waterloo to rejoin the path by the London Eye only about a mile from the Globe Theatre, our final destination. But don't forget - Shakespeare had to walk the whole way!*

The Slough Arm of the Grand Union Canal

Chapter 5   West Drayton to Shakespeare's Globe, London

(A) Back on the main route, having gone beneath the canal bridge at West Drayton. West Drayton Station visible over to right, beyond canal. It must have been near here that, in 1837, Brunel's steam locomotives were unloaded from barges, ready for the opening of his new Great Western Railway line. (*We now have a long and rather bland walk beside a straight and lock-free section of the Grand Union Canal as far as Norwood Top Lock - Para D below. Unless you wish to do otherwise, you can ignore route directions until reaching this - over six miles ahead.*) Under small hump-backed Horton Bridge, No. 193. Pass metal sign on left stating *Braunston 85 miles*. Under large concrete bridge and pass interesting, but defaced notice on left referring to *Grand Union Canal in Hillingdon*. Pass turn up left to the Woolpack Inn.

(B) Under Bridge No. 195 and under large concrete bridge just beyond. Pass large sand and gravel yard on right. Under small brick bridge overhung by trees. Under brick-built Dawley Bridge where canal starts to curve to right with poplar trees ahead, on right and path overhung by trees. Entry to Lake Farm Country Park on left. Under small concrete Bridge No. 199. Now passing more industrial buildings on right. Pass metal sign on left stating *Braunston 87 miles*. Go under medium-size Bridge No. 200. Pass The Old Crown Inn on left and path on left to Hayes and Harlington Station (*over bridge and walk southwards*). Veer left up surfaced path to go over hump-backed bridge crossing entry to small Hayes Dock on left. Under railway bridge and soon pass large Nestles factory over to right and under large concrete bridge beyond factory end, with path on left into Hillingdon.

(C) Over hump-backed Bull's Bridge crossing the Paddington Arm of the Grand Union Canal (*this was completed in 1801*) (SP - Brentford 6 miles). Pass large Tesco's supermarket over to right and colourful houseboats just beyond. Pass houses on immediate left and veer right to go off surfaced roadway and onto narrow towpath. Pass Grand Junction Arms on left and go under concrete bridge just beyond. Pass road lined with houses on left, recreation ground over to left, the Old Oak Tree Inn on left and under old brick Bridge No. 202. Over small bridge by entry to possibly deserted marina with colourful mosque visible from bridge, well over to left.

(D) Under large concrete bridge (*but turn up left and go over bridge if you wish to visit the Lamb Inn, visible over to right*). Pass Bixley Playingfield on left, pleasant mown lawns on left and

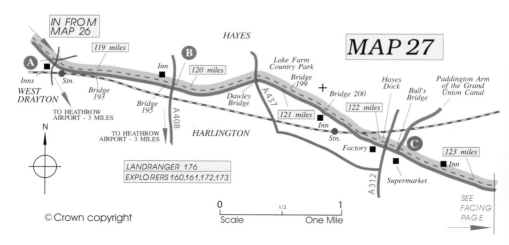

60

under footbridge before going over hump-backed bridge just beyond, crossing small waterway. Pass Top Lock Cottage on left and Norwood Top Lock (No. 90) on right. This is the first of eleven locks dropping down to the Thames, a group that includes the Hanwell Flight of locks. Now on pleasant towpath dropping down beside one more lock (No. 91) before passing broad meadow over to left. Under bridge and over railway line on aqueduct at the same time. *This is known as Windmill Bridge, or Three Bridges, and is a complex structure designed by Brunel to take his Great Western Railway line through a cutting under both the canal and the road.*

(E) Now descend the Hanwell Flight of locks (Nos. 92 - 97), with long brick wall to left with large hospital beyond. *Note bricked up archway in this wall - this was the entry to the Asylum Dock, where coal for the old mental hospital was unloaded. Note also the restored side-pond on the far side of the lock, opposite the*

Grand Union Canal east of Dawley Bridge - Green Corridor into London

archway; these ponds were for the conservation of water when the locks were opened. Over bridge crossing the River Brent, which comes in from left just before Lock 97 and which was utilised (or *canalised*) by the builders of the canal. Pass path to the Fox Inn down to left. (*It is possible to walk from here to Hanwell Station in about 15 minutes.*) Pass large warehouse on right and pass metal sign on left stating *Braunston 91 miles*. Under large bridge and pass pleasant green space to left with mown paths leading to park and with modern sculpture on skyline. Over bridge crossing entry to weir where River Brent temporarily leaves canal. Beyond weir pass Osterley Lock on right and picnic tables on left.

(F) Under very large bridge beneath M4 motorway at point where the River Brent re-joins the 'canal' and is again canalised. Under tall girder railway bridge. Approach elegant cast-iron 'roving' bridge (to allow horses to cross to opposite towpath) inscribed - *'Made at Horseley Ironworks near Birmingham 1820'* and turn right to cross it before turning left at its far end to go along towpath with canalised River Brent now to left. Pass weir over to left where River Brent leaves us again, with M4 going across bridge beyond, also to our left. Pass Clitheroes Lock on left, where River Brent re-joins us yet again and soon go under wooden foot-bridge. Keep on beside river as it broadens out, with modern buildings on both sides, noting especially the dramatic Glaxo-Smith-Klein building to left, with colourful metal sculpture in its riverside garden.

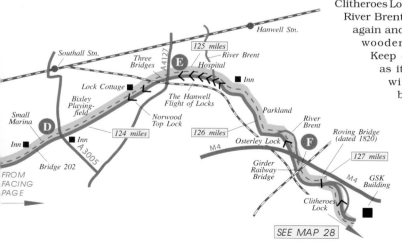

SEE MAP 28

(A) Under large concrete bridge carrying the A4 and under metal railway bridge. Turn right at start of large covered dock and almost immediately left to go along its right-hand side. Emerge onto pathway to right-hand side of extensive Brentford Basin, now with impressive flats over to left. Pass metal sign on left stating *Braunston 93 miles*. Near end of basin go over small steel swing-bridge and pass Brentford Gauging Locks

Thames Locks, where the Grand Union Canal joins the Thames

on immediate left. *The waterlines of all barges were permanently marked when unladen and this mark was compared with the waterline when loaded and this was the point where each loaded barge was measured (or gauged) to assess the toll to be paid before heading west and north to the Midlands.*

(B) Veer right, go up steps and then veer left **to go across busy A315 with great care - if traffic busy use pedestrian crossing**. *The route directions below may appear complex but take each one at a time and they will be easy to follow.* Leave road by going down steps at left-hand (eastern) end of bridge (SP - *Thames Path*). Go along path with River Brent to right. Ignore possible *Thames Path* sign to left by concrete steps, but keep along broad path. **With great care** go up metal steps to left where sign ahead indicates *No Exit Ahead* and continue in same direction on upper, paved path. Follow path as it zig-zags in front of flats to left, with River Brent still down to right. Go up concrete steps (SP - *Thames Path*) and on reaching large metal bridge ahead, turn left onto surfaced path and then turn sharp right to go beside road under bridge and immediately beyond bridge go up steps to immediate right of small garage workshop (SP - *Thames Path*). Go up steps onto bridge, cross River Brent and turn left and left again. Go down steps and, at bottom, turn right to go on path to immediate right of River Brent to approach Thames Locks. (*This is the point where the Grand Union Canal meets the tidal Thames and these locks can only be used for about two hours each side of high tide.*) Go to left of locks, climb two sections of steps immediately beyond and turn left to cross road bridge, the higher of the two. Go over second bridge, with weir to left and keep down paved roadway (Dock Road). *Having now left the Grand Union Canal, we shall follow the course of the River Thames as close as possible until journey's end at Shakespeare's Globe, using the Thames Path (henceforth coded as TP).*

(C) At end of Dock Road, turn right to go along pavement beside busy A315 (SP - *TP*). After about 70 paces turn right just before Heidelberg Building to go down narrow pathway with this building now on immediate left (SP - *TP*). Soon pass interesting boatyard down to right and just beyond, entrance to Thames Lock visible over to right. Turn left to go between large brick buildings on left and canalised entry to Brentford Arm of the Grand Union Canal on right. Pass Ferry Quays (luxury flats) on left and bear left by junction of canal with branch of the Thames over to right. Veer round to left and then turn right and right again (SP - *TP*) to pass Pappadums Restaurant and Bar up to left. Soon go straight, not left (SP - *TP*) with river still to immediate right. Pass building with glazed, semi-circular end and turn left to go up wide road (SP - *TP* and *Brentford High St*).

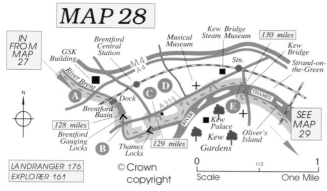

MAP 28

IN FROM MAP 27

GSK Building

River Brent

Brentford Central Station

M4 A4

Brentford Basin

128 miles

Brentford Gauging Locks

Dock

Thames Locks

129 miles

A315

RIVER

Musical Museum

Kew Bridge Steam Museum

Stn.

Kew Palace

Kew Gardens

Oliver's Island

THAMES

130 miles

Kew Bridge

Strand-on-the-Green

SEE MAP 29

N

LANDRANGER 176
EXPLORER 161

© Crown copyright

0   1/2   1
Scale   One Mile

(D) At top of road turn right to go along pavement beside busy A315 and after about 130 paces turn right just short of traffic lights at junction with B455 (SP - *TP* and *Smith Hill*). At bottom of steps turn left through fenced gap and immediately right by edge of car parking area. Down short path before turning left with Thames now again on right. On reaching glazed doors ahead turn left and left again to go up steps before turning left yet again. Now keep along raised pathway which soon drops down to pass gardens on left (*Waterman's Park - but not signed at this end*). Good view ahead of the old Kew Pumping Station Tower (*see below*). *Housed in the tower of the old St George's Church over to left, is the Musical Museum, with its fascinating collection of automatic pianos and various organs.* At end of Waterman's Park gardens, go up steps and turn right onto pavement beside busy A315 (SP - *Kew Bridge*). After about 80 paces turn right immediately beyond Captain Morgan's (pub) and at bottom of steps turn left to go along narrow path with Thames just to right, but obscured by shrubs and bushes.

(E) On meeting Kew Bridge turn left away from river (SP - *Kew Bridge Station*) and up surfaced roadway. After about 60 paces go up stone steps and turn right and right again to join pavement on right-hand side of busy A205 road to cross Kew Bridge. *(But turn left if you wish to visit Kew Bridge Steam Museum, which is housed in the old Kew Pumping Station. This formerly pumped water from the Thames to the homes of west London and to the Regents Canal and although now replaced with electric power, its five massive Cornish pumping-engines are still kept in working order, along with an amount of other pumping machines. Well worth visiting.)* Back on the main route crossing Kew Bridge - Well before meeting small bus shelter ahead, turn right and immediately left to go down stone steps. At bottom of steps turn right and after 40 paces turn right onto the Thames Path with river now to immediate left (SP - *Chiswick Bridge*). Soon pass Kew Gardens Pier on left and keep along path overhung by trees. Good views across river to Strand- on-the- Green, with its attractive houses, which were once fishermen's cottages. Pass small, wooded Oliver's Island, over to left.

Kew Bridge

(A) Just beyond Oliver's Island, go under iron-girder Kew Railway Bridge, noting its handsome brick abutment ornamented by stone pillars and carved capitals. Keep along very pleasant riverside path shaded by trees, but **keep eyes and ears open for cyclists that share it with you!** Pass, over to left, the back of the National Archive, previously known as the Public Record Office. Pass luxury flats well over to right. Entrance to Chiswick Quay Marina over to left. Pass Putney Town Rowing Club on right. Now pass through more open stretch with grassy space to right, but still overhung with trees. Handsome stone-built Chiswick Bridge visible ahead.

(B) Walk beneath Chiswick Bridge passing small green on right and keep on path parallel with road just to right. The riverbank opposite is tree-lined between here and Barnes, this being the edge of the large open space of Duke's Meadow with its sports field, golf course etc.. Pass the Ship Inn on right - *this marks the finishing point of the annual Oxford and Cambridge Boat Race, the start being at Putney Bridge, some 4 miles and 374 yards ahead. After we too have rounded the great `Hammersmith Bend` we shall certainly appreciate the skills of the boats' coxes in addition to the fortitude of their crews.* Beyond the Ship Inn go

along short section of road before veering left to go on an inferior quality path in front of the old Mortlake Brewery - a rather forbidding, dark brick building. (*Note: This next section of path can sometimes be flooded at exceptionally high tides - If this appears to be a possibility, turn right just beyond the Ship Inn and go 'inland' to use a length of Mortlake High Street before returning to the riverside well before Barnes.*) Pass old walls to right which shield us from the newer Stag Brewery buildings and along cobbled path noting old railway line that used to go into the brewery from a wharf here. Go across lower cobbled area, the section most

The Ship Inn, Mortlake

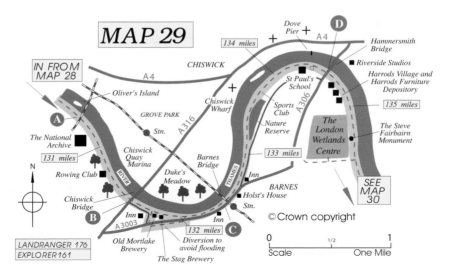

MAP 29

IN FROM MAP 28

Oliver's Island

CHISWICK

A4

Dove Pier

A4

D

Hammersmith Bridge

134 miles

Riverside Studios

St Paul's School

Harrods Village and Harrods Furniture Depository

A

The National Archive

131 miles

GROVE PARK

Stn.

Chiswick Wharf

A306

Chiswick Quay Marina

Rowing Club

Chiswick Bridge

Duke's Meadow

Sports Club

Nature Reserve

The London Wetlands Centre

135 miles

The Steve Fairbairn Monument

N

Barnes Bridge

133 miles

SEE MAP 30

Inn

BARNES

Holst's House

Stn.

B

Inn

A3003

Inn

132 miles

C

© Crown copyright

LANDRANGER 176
EXPLORER 161

Old Mortlake Brewery

Diversion to avoid flooding

The Stag Brewery

0   1/2   1
Scale   One Mile

vulnerable to flooding and continue on often muddy path. Pass flats on right and Barnes Railway Bridge now visible ahead. Pass Ye White Hart Inn on right and now going parallel with busy road to right (*where those using the 'inland diversion' along Mortlake High Street would re-join this main route*).

Barnes Bridge

(C) Go on raised concrete path under Barnes Bridge and keep on this raised path to immediate left of busy road, passing a series of pretty late 18th- and early 19th-century houses on right. *These include one with a blue plaque noting that the composer Gustav Holst lived here between 1908 and 1913, when he was Director of Music at St Paul's School for Girls.* Pass turning on right to Barnes High Street and the Bull's Head Inn just beyond on our right, continuing on raised concrete path beside road. Soon veer left at end of concrete path and go onto path beneath trees nearest to riverbank. Nature Reserve over to our right is based on an old reservoir. Pass Chiswick Wharf over to left with Chiswick Church just beyond and many pleasant houses in their vicinity. Pass sports club on right. Pass buildings and playing fields of St Paul's School on right - these are on the site of a filled-in reservoir. Pass boathouse on right with an open space looking across to Dove Pier. *Impressively ornate Hammersmith Bridge visible ahead. This is the triumphant*

Hammersmith Bridge

design of Sir Joseph Bazalgette, the great engineer to whom we owe so much, especially for his construction of London's massive sewerage system.

The old Harrods Furniture Depository building

(D) **Go with care on path below Hammersmith Bridge - it has very little headroom.** Riverside Studios visible across river to left and many large, modern flats on riverbank beyond. Soon pass the beginning of Harrods Village on right. This is based around the extravagantly ornamented Harrods Furniture Depository building, which has itself been converted into flats. Pass the banks of the Barn Elms Reservoirs on right. These have been converted into The London Wetlands Centre - for details see page 66. *Pass small stone monument on right. This commemorates Steve Fairbairn (1862-1938), the famous oarsman and coach who founded the Head of the River Race. This is one mile from the start of the University Boat Race Course at Putney.* Putney Bridge now visible well ahead. Pass sign on right depicting two flying swans, indicating the outer boundary of the Wetlands Centre.

Boat Race shore above Putney Bridge

(A) Just beyond sign with flying swans, keep straight on at path junction (SP - *Putney*), ignoring turning on right (but turn right along Queen Elizabeth's Walk if you wish to visit the London Wetlands Centre, its main entrance being only 700 yards away). *The London Wetlands Centre has been created on the 105-acre site of the old Barnes Reservoirs and, with its 170 species of wild birds, more than 300 butterflies and moths and a host of other creatures, is well worth visiting.* Fulham Football Club's stadium visible well over to left. Pass extensive sports fields over to right. Pass Barn Elms Boathouse and South Bank Sailing Club, both on right. Over small bridge crossing the Beverley Brook which has flowed across Wimbledon Common and Richmond Park before joining the Thames here. Now go onto wide path beside road to right, at our entry to Putney. Trees lining bank opposite conceal the grounds of Fulham Palace. *Until 1973 this had been the Bishop of London's residence for over a thousand years.* At end of path walk along left-hand edge of road with care and pass several rowing club boathouses over to right. *Good views ahead of the handsome, stone-built Putney Bridge which, like Hammersmith Bridge, was designed by Sir Joseph Bazalgette.* Pass riverbank sloping down to left. *This is near the starting point of the Oxford and Cambridge Boat Race.* Go along tree-lined path and pass Duke's Head and Star and Garter Restaurant, both on right. Pass Putney Pier on left and the Putney Bridge Restaurant on right. Now veer left to go on pavement beside left-hand side of busier road. Church tower visible ahead, dwarfed by monstrous flats. *From here onwards we shall miss the simplicity and ease of the old Thames towpath, which no longer exists below Putney.*

(B) At road junction to immediate south of Putney Bridge use controlled crossing to go over busy A219, initially aiming for the tower of St Mary the Virgin's Church. Turn right beyond crossing and immediately turn left beyond church. Turn left again and then right, to go beside Thames with massive flats to right. Go round to right of slipway soon passing Boathouse Inn over to right. Keep along riverside path and at its end, turn right, away from river. On arriving at road veer left across it and turn left into Deodar Road. Keep down this road on left-hand pavement, going under Putney Railway Bridge (*there is a good link across this bridge to Putney Bridge Tube Station*) and eventually pass handsome Thornhill House on right-hand side.

(C) Just beyond Thornhill House, at end of Deodar Road, go straight across it (SP - *Riverside Walk*) and beneath large archway and cross paved area between flats of Blade Mews. Go through smaller archway into Wandsworth Park and veer left to walk beside the Thames on path overhung with fine trees. *Good view across Thames to the tree-lined Hurlingham Club, with its elegant 18th-century house. Also good views ahead of Wandsworth Bridge.* At end of park keep straight through gate onto Lighterman's Wharf, passing flats on right and Prospect Quay on left. Turn right, away from river, just beyond Ghillies Restaurant. (*It **may***

be possible to keep along river bank at some time in the future.)

(D) Turn left at road junction into Britannia Row immediately before meeting railway bridge (SP - *Wandle Delta Creek*). Pass offices on left, bear left by Bernard Thorpe's offices on left and almost immediately turn right, into Enterprise Way with commercial buildings on both sides. At its end veer slightly right to go over footbridges crossing two

Low tide just east of Wandsworth Park

branches of the River Wandle, noting sign on left stating that a tidal mill stood here from medieval times until demolished in 1892. *This river was mentioned in Isaac Walton's Compleat Angler, as a good trout stream and he would no doubt be delighted to learn that the once highly-polluted, but now much cleaner Wandle has recently rewarded an enterprising fly fisherman with a catch.* Now keep along pavement on left-hand side of road known as Smugglers' Way. Pass very large re-cycling plant on left **taking care to keep out of the way of the many heavy lorries visiting it**. Vast quantities of rubbish are put into containers here and loaded onto barges for transport down river.

(E) At end of re-cycling plant turn left off road to go on path (SP - *TP*) with new flats to right. Turn right onto Nickols Walk with Thames now again on left (*this may be the point where an extended path comes in from left - see Ghillies Restaurant, above*). Good view ahead of unusually clad Wandsworth Bridge, not the most elegant of the Thames Bridges! Pass luxury flats on right and at end of Nickols Way turn right, away from river and right again by Al Ponte Restaurant (SP - *TP*). Now turn left, to go behind Ship Inn and turn right just beyond it. Now go left along Jews Row and at its top turn right to go along pavement beside

very busy A217, with traffic going to and from Wandsworth Bridge, along to our left. At large traffic gyratory turn left to use controlled crossing **with great care** and go left again to go beside A3205, York Road (SP - *Central London*). Pass Battersea Reach flats on left. Pass service station on left and soon turn left along Mendip Road (SP - *TP*). At end of Mendip Road turn right into Chatfield Road and after 30 paces turn left to go up across Mendip Court.

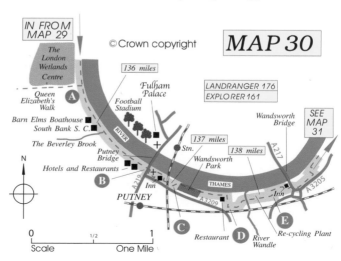

MAP 30

IN FROM MAP 29

The London Wetlands Centre

136 miles

Fulham Palace

LANDRANGER 176
EXPLORER 161

Queen Elizabeth's Walk **(A)**

Football Stadium

Wandsworth Bridge

SEE MAP 31

Barn Elms Boathouse
South Bank S. C.

RIVER

The Beverley Brook

137 miles

Stn.

138 miles

A217

Putney Bridge

Wandsworth Park

N

Hotels and Restaurants

A219

(B)

THAMES

A3205

Inn

PUTNEY

A3209

Inn

0   1/2   1
Scale   One Mile

(C)

Restaurant **(D)**

River Wandle

Re-cycling Plant **(E)**

67

(A) Now turn right beyond Mendip Court to regain broad riverside path, with Thames to left and flats to right. Pass the impressive flats of Plantation Wharf on right and just beyond circular glass building, turn right, away from river and go along pathway with flats to right. Turn left to go across car parking area and at its end turn left to go along pavement beside busy A3205, York Road, with first large car showroom on left. Just beyond second large

Lots Road Power Station

car showroom on left, turn left onto Lombard Road (SP - *TP*). Keep on left-hand pavement bearing right by entry to Heliport on left and pass more flat developments (Oyster Wharf) on left. Go under railway bridge and immediately turn left (SP - *TP*), initially going parallel with railway line.

(B) Now turn right to regain riverside path with good view of railway bridge back to left and colourful moored barges alongside.. Now passing luxurious Chelsea Harbour development beyond Thames to left. Go along path with river to left and flats to right. Substantial brick-built Lots Road Power Station ahead left - this still provides electric power for London's Underground Railway system. Now running parallel with road visible over to right. Pass slipway down to left and go straight through gates into churchyard of the elegant little St Mary's Church, Battersea, with its handsome portico and small spire. *What a splendid contrast with much of the area through which we are passing.* Keep straight through churchyard and resume walk beside river passing impressive glass-fronted buildings on right. Post Office Tower just briefly visible on skyline ahead. Now going along Morgan's Walk and at its end bear slightly right passing bronze statue of man, woman and child by John Ravera.

(C) Over busy A3220 road **with great care** with Battersea Bridge to left and then bear left to go down steps between bronze sculpture of two impressive flying geese. Keep straight ahead on paved riverside walk with flats to right. Good views ahead of the elegantly designed and ornamented Albert Bridge. Pass the Thames sailing barge *Atrato* on left. *This was built in 1898 at Wivenhoe, Essex and ended her working days in 1980.* Pass dramatic flats on right- a little stark but they

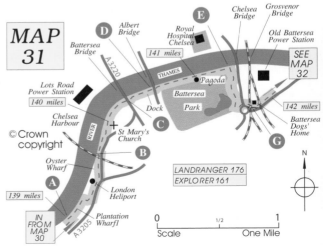

complement the Albert Bridge well. Cross narrow dock entry with a sluice gate. On meeting Albert Bridge go up steps and read notice on left stating that *all troops must break step when marching over* - reminding us that despite its attractions, this bridge is not as strong as its designer would have wished.

St Mary's Church, Battersea

(D) Now cross road **with care** by using traffic island down to right before veering left and entering Battersea Park. *Once a marshy area, this park was created in 1854 by using vast quantities of earth, brought from newly excavated docks.* Veer left to go along broad pathway beside river, with most of the large Battersea Park over to right. Chelsea Bridge soon visible ahead. Pass pleasant ornamental pond over to right, complete with many playing fountains. Pass the impressive and entirely unexpected London Peace Pagoda on right. *This was the seventieth pagoda built throughout the world by the Buddhist Nipponzan Myohojii Order and was presented by them to London in 1985. It is over 100 feet high and has gilded statues of Buddha in niches on its four sides.*

(E) At end of riverside walk, with Chelsea Bridge just ahead, bear right, up pathway and veer slightly left to cross roadway in Battersea Park. *(In years to come the Thames Path will continue along the riverside (probably first using an underpass beneath Chelsea Bridge) all the way from here to Vauxhall Bridge (see below) - We hope to provide update sheets covering any future improvements.)* Go down gently curving path (SP - *TP*) and soon turn right and then left at junction of paths beneath tree. Pass athletic ground on right and take next turn left, away from athletic ground fence (SP - *TP*). Almost immediately bear right and then bear left to follow curving path with wooden fence to left. At end of path turn left onto roadway and after 30 paces go out through gates leaving Battersea Park and turn left to go half-way round Queen's Circus. Cross Queenstown Road **with great care** and bear right.

The Albert Bridge

(F) But then turn left to go on pavement under railway bridge (SP - *Elephant and Castle*) and along Prince of Wales Drive. Bear left to go beside busy A3205 (Battersea Park Road), go under railway bridge, pass Battersea Dogs' Home on left (*This famous and much respected institution was founded in 1860 as 'a temporary home for lost and starving dogs'. Did you know that it has also been taking cats since 1882?*).

(A) Beyond Battersea Dogs' Home go over yet another railway bridge. Old Battersea Power Station visible over wall to left. Pass Sleaford Street Bus Stop and turn left at cross-roads into Kirtling Street (SP - *TP*), which soon bears to right by entrance to old Battersea Power Station on left. Over cross-roads crossing Cringle Street and turn right at end of Kirtling Street (SP - *TP*). After about 90 paces turn left up path with wall to left and hedge to right (SP - *TP*). Turn right onto Tideway Walk, with river now to immediate left. Pass Nine Elms Pier to left, turn right, then left to go round small dock with moored boats. Turn left again and then right to return briefly to riverside. Soon turn right by entry to Battersea Barge Restaurant on left and down path away from river.

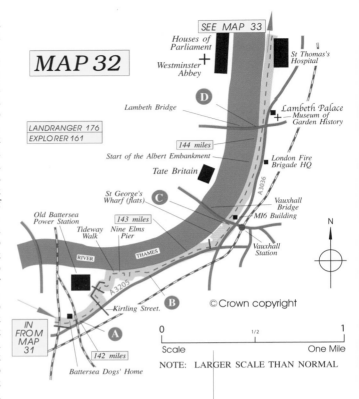

MAP 32

SEE MAP 33

Houses of Parliament

Westminster Abbey

St Thomas's Hospital

LANDRANGER 176
EXPLORER 161

Lambeth Bridge

D

Lambeth Palace
Museum of Garden History

144 miles

Start of the Albert Embankment

Tate Britain

London Fire Brigade HQ

St George's Wharf (flats)

C

Vauxhall Bridge

Old Battersea Power Station

143 miles

MI6 Building

N

Tideway Walk

Nine Elms Pier

RIVER

THAMES

Vauxhall Station

A3036

A3205

Kirtling Street.

B

© Crown copyright

IN FROM MAP 31

A

142 miles

Battersea Dogs' Home

0   1/2   1

Scale   One Mile

NOTE: LARGER SCALE THAN NORMAL

(B) Now turn left to go on pavement beside busy A3205 (Nine Elms Road) and after about 100 paces turn left (SP - *TP*) and then right, again returning to riverside - now on William Henry Walk. Pass pleasantly mature flats on right. Brief glimpse of the London Eye ahead left, revealing how far the Thames curves away beyond here. Pass tree-shaded, grassy strip on right and at end of this riverside walk turn right and almost immediately turn left to again

View northwards to Lambeth Bridge

go along pavement beside busy A3205 road for a short distance. (*Eventually the Thames Path will go straight ahead in front of St George's Wharf Flats (many still to be built), keeping to immediate right of river bank.*) Then turn right to go over minor road by traffic lights. At next traffic lights, turn left into A3036 (SP - *TP*). After about 300 paces bear left by roundabout (with Vauxhall Tube Station over to right), to keep along pavement beside A202 towards Vauxhall Bridge. But just before crossing bridge, turn left, down steps

The Houses of Parliament from Lambeth Bridge

(SP - TP). (*It will be at this point that the future Thames Path will come in from left, but this may be some years ahead.*) Immediately turn sharp right to go through underpass beneath A202.

(C) Immediately beyond underpass, veer slightly left to go along riverside walk passing the architecturally questionable MI6 building on right, fronted by its row of fountains. *The London Eye now a dramatic feature of the view ahead.* Turn right by gazebo at its end and after about 40 paces turn left, go over road to slipway down to left, turn left again and then turn right to return to riverside walk. *Good views of the Houses of Parliament ahead left.* Pass large building on right fronted by mown lawn and at its end, with ever narrowing grass strip to right, along the start of the impressive Albert Embankment, built in 1866-69 by the noted engineer, Sir Joseph Bazalgette, some of whose works we have already encountered. The busy A3036 road now alongside on right. Pass London Fire Brigade HQ on right. *Tate Britain visible over to left, across the Thames. Also note bronze ship's prow projecting from offices over to right.*

(D) Go through underpass beneath Lambeth Bridge and pass Lambeth Pier on left. Lambeth Palace, with its mellow-brick Tudor gatehouse across road to right. *This was built by Henry VIII's Cardinal Archbishop Henry Morton. `The dole` was handed out to the local poor at the gatehouse until the mid-19th century. The Great Hall, behind it, was built in 1663 and was described by Samuel Pepys as `a new old-fashioned hall'.* **Cross road to right with great care** *if you wish to look at the Palace's exterior or visit the adjacent Museum of Garden History in the old Parish Church of St Mary, with its cemetery now a garden but appropriately still containing the family tomb of the Tradescants, the well-known 17th-century royal gardeners and plant hunters.*

Archbishop Morton's Gatehouse, Lambeth Palace

Note the usually large number of tourists taking in the view across the river to the Houses of Parliament, with the towers of Westminster Abbey just briefly visible behind, to their left. Keep along straight stretch of Albert Embankment, here backed by the vast and extensively modernised buildings of St Thomas's Hospital. *Founded in the early 12th century this famous hospital moved from Southwark in 1856 and it was soon after this that Florence Nightingale established her School of Nursing here.*

(A) Just before the end of the Albert Embankment look left for fine view of Big Ben with Westminster Bridge leading towards it. Note the large lion on its plinth above us - this came from the Lion Brewery, which was demolished to make way for the Festival of Britain Exhibition of 1951, the site being now occupied by the Royal Festival Hall (see below).

Now turn right and immediately left to go through underpass beneath Westminster Bridge. Go along the Queen's Walk in front of the old County Hall Building, now housing two hotels, an art gallery and an aquarium. Pass to the right of the base of the London Eye with large green space to our right known as Jubilee Gardens. Continue along the Queen's Walk with Thames to immediate left and Jubilee Gardens over to right.

(B) Go beneath Hungerford Railway Bridge with the Golden Jubilee footways alongside it, allowing a river crossing for pedestrians. We are now in the area known as the South Bank, all of which was cleared for the 1951 Festival of Britain. Only one of its buildings has survived and we now pass this - the Royal Festival Hall. Added later, the Queen Elizabeth Hall and the Purcell Room are both to our right, by the side of the Festival Hall. The Festival Pier is to our left and the Hayward Gallery is visible over to right. These monolithic concrete buildings have little warmth about them, but despite their architectural shortcomings, the area around and within them is full of life, especially in the evenings.

(C) Go beneath the concrete but, in this case, very elegant Waterloo Bridge, with the National Film Theatre on right, tucked away beneath the bridge. Pass the National Theatre complex on right, comprising the Olivier, the Lyttleton and the Cottesloe. St Paul's Cathedral now visible ahead left. Pass interesting viewing indicator by railings on left. Veer slightly right and pass Gabriel's Wharf - a welcoming plaza with restaurants and shops down to right and the Bernie Spain Gardens just beyond on right. Go along partly-covered walkway alongside the Oxo Building with the Oxo Tower above it, the latter being not easily discernible from our path. Pass Sea Containers House (a large office block) on right and Doggett's Coat and Badge Restaurant on right. *The colourful Doggett's Coat and Badge has, since 1715, been awarded annually to the winner of a single sculls race for apprentice watermen.* Toilets down to left.

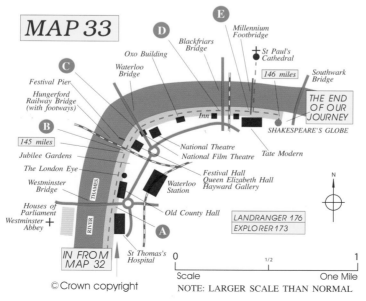

(D) Go through long underpass beneath Blackfriars Bridge, *noting interesting giant enlargements of engravings illustrating this bridge's history. These include the alternative designs for the original bridge of 1756 followed by engravings of the bridge at various stages in its building. Now note proud and very colourful cast-iron crest of the London, Chatham and Dover Railway up to left before going through underpass beneath this long closed*

company's bridge. Continue on broad walkway, known as Bankside, with fine view of St Paul's Cathedral now over to left. Veer right to go behind the Founder's Arms and now pass, on right, the massive building, once the Bankside Power Station, designed by Sir Giles Gilbert Scott, and now housing the art gallery - Tate Modern. Do not miss a visit here - the architectural conversion of its massive

Shakespeare's Globe - our final destination

interior is truly amazing and the ever-changing displays of modern art are always challenging.

(E) Now go beneath the dramatic Millennium Bridge, a footbridge leading across the Thames, with a vista of St Paul's beyond it. Despite its initial vibration problems, it is a stunning piece of engineering design and a great addition to Bankside. Situated between today's Blackfriars and Southwark Bridges, Bankside encompassed a maze of narrow streets and alleys and was notorious for its theatres, riotous taverns, brothels, bear- and bull-baiting and cockfighting. Disowned by the staid citizens to the north of the Thames, much of this area was owned by the Bishops of Winchester, the local prostitutes being known as *Winchester Geese*. To explore the area in detail read Nick Robins' excellent guide *Walking Shakespeare's London*, which is available in the Shakespeare's Globe bookshop. Pass the Cardinal's Wharf area, with its cobbled close down to right with the Provost of Southwark Cathedral's Lodge and the small mellow brick house beside it, which is thought to have been used by Sir Christopher Wren, when supervising the building of St Paul's. Just beyond these houses turn right to arrive at one of the entrances to Shakespeare's Globe, thus completing our 146-mile journey from Shakespeare's Stratford-upon-Avon.

Built some 200 yards from the site of the original Globe Theatre, Shakespeare's Globe was the brainchild of the visionary American actor and director, Sam Wanamaker and was opened in 1997. Sadly Sam died before the work was completed, but the story of his persistent struggles and that of his team of scholars, architects, craftsmen, staff and supporters, to achieve their objective is movingly told in the all-year-round exhibition housed in the great Under-Globe beneath the theatre. Here is the world's largest exhibition devoted to Shakespeare and the London in which he worked and lived and it brings Shakespeare's world to life using a range of interactive displays and live demonstrations. The brilliant design of the open-air theatre above is based on the scanty sources of information on the original Globe and its neighbouring theatres, the Swan, the Rose and the Hope. A visit to the exhibition and to the theatre above, probably taking one and a half hours, would be a fitting end to your long journey, but naturally, if you're walking between May and October, you will also wish to attend a performance on the Globe's historic stage.

Congratulations on completing your journey. We hope you have enjoyed it all. **If you feel like making a small contribution to the Shakespeare Hospice of Stratford-upon-Avon, for the support of which Shakespeare's Way was established and continues to be maintained, it would be much appreciated.** Your contribution will be forwarded to them without any deduction and your generosity and that of any sponsoring friends and relations will be acknowledged. If you would like a certificate recording our congratulations on your achievement and our thanks for your contribution, do ask for one. Write to The Shakespeare's Way Association, St Mary's Barn, Pillerton Priors, Warwick CV35 0PG.

A LIST OF TOWNS AND VILLAGES ON SHAKESPEARE'S WAY WITH MILEAGES FROM STRATFORD-UPON-AVON AND SHAKESPEARE'S GLOBE, LONDON

Stratford-upon-Avon	0	146	Britwell Salome	76	70
Clifford Chambers	3	143	Cookley Green	81	65
Preston-on-Stour	4	142	Maidensgrove	83	63
Alderminster	7	139	Stonor	85	61
Ettington Park	9	137	Hambleden	90	56
Halford	11	135	Marlow	96	50
Honington	15	131	Bourne End	99	47
Shipston-on-Stour	17	129	Cookham	100	46
Willington	18	128	Hedsor	102	44
Cherington	21	125	Burnham Beeches	106	40
Long Compton	24	122	Farnham Common	107	39
Little Rollright	27	119	Fulmer	110	36
Salford	29	117	Iver	116	30
Chipping Norton	31	115	West Drayton	119	27
Enstone	36	110	Bull's Bridge	122	24
Cleveley	37	109	Hanwell Locks	125	21
Ditchley Park	40	106	Thames Lock, Brentford	129	17
Blenheim Park	45	101	Kew Bridge	130	16
Woodstock	47	99	Chiswick Bridge	131	15
Bladon	48	98	Barnes Bridge	132	14
Yarnton	52	94	Hammersmith Bridge	134	12
Wolvercote	54	92	Putney Bridge	137	9
Oxford	58	88	Wandsworth Bridge	138	8
Sandford-on-Thames	62	84	Battersea Bridge	140	6
Toot Baldon	65	81	Chelsea Bridge	141	5
Marsh Baldon	66	80	Vauxhall Bridge	143	3
Chiselhampton	68	78	Lambeth Bridge	144	2
Stadhampton	69	77	Westminster Bridge	144	2
Chalgrove	71	75	Waterloo Bridge	145	1
Brightwell Baldwin	74	72	Shakespeare's Globe	146	0

Shakespeare's Early Years

William Shakespeare was born in April 1564 at the house of his parents, John and Mary, in Henley Street, Stratford-upon-Avon. Although later falling on hard times, John was a prosperous glover and wool dealer and had, in 1568, held the office of Bailiff or mayor of the Borough. His wife Mary was the daughter of a yeoman farmer of nearby Wilmcote. It is believed that William was educated at the town's grammar school and it is certain that in November 1582, when he was 18, he married a 26-year old widow, Anne Hathaway, of Shottery, then just outside the town. No doubt Anne was already pregnant when the marriage took place and in May of the following year, their daughter, Susannah was born. In February 1585 Anne produced twins, Hamnet and Judith.

William Shakespeare - the posthumous engraving by Martin Droeshout in the first folio of 1623

When did Shakespeare, the young father, first set out for London, and why? There have been many attempts to answer these questions, but the period between 1585 and 1592, by which time the poet was well established in London, are known to all Shakespearian scholars as `The Lost Years`. Some feel that Shakespeare, already fascinated by the performances of various companies of strolling players, simply fell in with one of them and travelled with them to London as part of their group. Others think that he left to avoid punishment for riotous behaviour in local inns, or for poaching deer from neighbouring Charlecote Park. A further theory has been advanced; in that he may have left Stratford to avoid any possible connection with the highly dangerous activities of Roman Catholic plotters. This remains a possibility when we recall that 1588 was the year of the Spanish Armada, when Philip of Spain hoped to unseat Queen Elizabeth and re-impose Roman Catholicism. But what is certain is that by 1592 Shakespeare had already gained some experience as an actor

Bankside in 1647 - an extract from Wenceslaus Hollar's `Long View of London'. The labels have been reversed: the 'Beere bayting' is the Globe and 'The Globe' is the Hope, a dual-purpose animal baiting ring and theatre.

and a reviser of plays. He joined the company of players who entertained the Court and his plays were already being performed at the Theatre and Curtain Playhouse in Shoreditch and at the Rose. Soon after this he and a small group of friends built and managed the Globe Theatre and he was writing the plays that brought him wealth and success, but let us look back to his first journey to London and to the journeys that followed, as these are the basis of our `Shakespeare's Way`.

Shakespeare's Journeys

With no certainties available, it would appear likely, on the scanty evidence above, that Shakespeare first journeyed to London some time between 1585 and 1588. On this first of many journeys between Stratford and the capital, he may have travelled alone, or he may have travelled with a company of strolling players. He may have ridden a horse but this would have incurred the costs of stabling and feed, and the possibility of hiring charges and it is more likely that he made the less expensive choice and journeyed on foot. However it seems likely that he stopped more than once at the Crown Inn in Oxford which was owned by his friend, John Davenant. We have therefore planned a direct route between Stratford and Oxford. This crosses part of the Cotswolds, referred to in Shakespeare's play, *Richard II*, as `these high wild hills and rough uneven ways`. It also passes close to the Rollright Stones with their legendary king and witch and, up here on a bleak winter's day, it takes little imagination to picture the impressionable young poet storing up his experience for future use. Macbeth's Three Witches immediately come to mind.

Anne Hathaway's Cottage, Shottery

A view down the Avon to Holy Trinity Church, Stratford-upon-Avon, Shakespeare's burial place

And so to Oxford, to arrive at the site of the Davenants' Crown Inn, the ground floor of which is now occupied by a betting shop. The frequently unreliable 17th-century gossip, John Aubrey, relates in his *Brief Lives* that Shakespeare `was wont to go into Warwickshire once a year, and did in his journey lye at this house in Oxon where he was exceedingly respected`. In 1606, Shakespeare is said to have become godfather to the Davenants' second son, William, who later

The River Thames below Godstow, looking across to Port Meadow (see page 32)

became a playright himself and who was made Poet Laureate in 1636. Aubrey also states that William Davenant's mother `was a very beautiful woman' and that later in life, over a glass or two of wine, Davenant hinted that he was Shakespeare's natural son, thereby maligning his poor, long-departed mother.

By a happy chance Samuel Schoenbaum in his invaluable book, *William Shakespeare - A Compact Documentary Life*, favours the Stratford-Oxford route that we had planned before reading it. However he thinks that beyond Oxford, Shakespeare would have probably gone via High Wycombe and Beaconsfield. This would appear very likely, but as the poet would then have followed a route now taken by that of the M40 we felt that a more tranquil southern alternative was preferable. This alternative also has the merit of arriving at the fringes of London at the point where the Grand Union Canal enters it and we have chosen this very un-Elizabethan highway as our best option. Shakespeare would almost certainly have journeyed through Uxbridge, a little to the canal's north but, like us, he may have gone through Brentford and then, although unlikely, he might have used at least part of the Thames towpath on his final stage to London's Bankside.

It is not known how much time Shakespeare spent in Stratford-upon-Avon in the years after his first journey to London in about 1585. He does not appear to have stayed for long at any one time although he may have returned briefly each year to see something of Anne and his children. Hamnet his boy twin died in 1596 and only a year later the poet had become prosperous enough to buy New Place, one of Stratford's largest houses. Despite this purchase he must have continued to spend most of his time in London and he probably continued to journey back and forth at intervals, now almost certainly on horseback. He did eventually return to live at New Place permanently, probably in about 1610, and he died here in 1616 at the age of 52. He was buried in Stratford-upon-Avon's Holy Trinity Church, where his grave and monument may still be seen.

In the Great Garden of New Place, Shakespeare's last home

INDEX

ACKNOWLEDGEMENTS AND THANKS

During the establishment of Shakespeare's Way and the compilation of the two guides describing it, we have received much help and advice. We are especially indebted to the teams of walkers who have waymarked the path in both directions, and who have carefully checked our route directions. Our thanks also to the officers of the counties through which the path passes, all of whom have shown patience, understanding and encouragement. Parish Clerks along the route have also been most helpful in providing details of land occupancy.

We should also like to thank the vast majority of occupiers of the land over which Shakespeare's Way passes, who have dealt with our enquiries and some might feel, our intrusions, in a tolerant and friendly manner.

Inevitably we shall miss some names, but may we record our grateful thanks to all those who have helped in so many different ways including ....

...... Jenny Beardmore, Robert Bearman, Roger & Kathy Benson, Derek and Kathy Bingham, Tony Clarke, Richard Dick, Ruth Elliot, Stephen Fox, Sarah Golding, Hilary Hargreaves, Lionel Howse, Denis Keyte, Len Lamb, Rebecca McNaught, Hugh Potter, John Roberts, Nick Robins, Andrew Swann, Joanne Taylor, Dan Weeks, Tony Wilson and also several members of the invaluable Chiltern Society. The Society welcomes new members. If you would like to join, please write to them at: White Hill Centre, White Hill, Chesham, Bucks HP5 1AG

SHAKESPEARE'S WAY PUBLICATIONS
Write or phone 01789 740852 for prices, or see our web site www.shakespearesway.org

SHAKESPEARE'S WAY - The 80-page main guidebook to Shakespeare's Way FROM Stratford-upon-Avon TO Shakespeare's Globe, London. With descriptive text, and coloured illustrations and maps.

THE EAST-WEST SUPPLEMENT - The 32-page guide providing route directions only, starting at Shakespeare's Globe and finishing at Stratford-upon-Avon.

THE SHAKESPEARE'S WAY PLANNER - The 8-page guide providing details of accommodation and meals facilities along the route of Shakespeare's Way.

UPDATE SHEET FOR THE MAIN GUIDEBOOK .... No Charge

These publications are available from The Shakespeare's Way Association, St Mary's Barn, Pillerton Priors, Warwick CV35 0PG. We regret that we cannot accept credit or debit cards. Cheques to The Shakespeare's Way Association, please.